My HOPE Story

Volume Two

hope✳books collaborations

Published by hope*books

2217 Matthews Township Pkwy

Suite D302

Matthews, NC 28105

www.hopebooks.com

hope*books is a division of hope*media

Printed in the United States of America

First paperback edition.

Paperback ISBN: 979-8-89185-411-6

Hardcover ISBN: 979-8-89185-362-1

Ebook ISBN: 979-8-89185-363-8

Library of Congress Number: 2026935294

hb
hope✸books

Table of Contents

Foreword

By Brian Dixon

Stories of hope remind us that God is still writing our stories. Each written word within the following pages testify to a hope that does not disappoint. The lives each of these women live and the stories they tell, bear witness to the truth of God's character and the steady promise of hope that we have in him. As Romans 5:3-5 teaches, suffering produces perseverance, perseverance, character, and character hope.

Even in a psych ward, in the midst of sexual abuse, in fear, despair, bitterness, perfectionism, death...In all these things, God remains. He enters into the middle of it all to bring His goodness, healing, mercy, and joy.

My prayer for you as you read is to see your own story reflected back. Pause, remember how God has held you in His arms. Your story is not too much, too difficult. Your story is a part of His redemption.

May this book offer a reminder that God entered into humanity, walked, preached, prayed, wrote in the sand. He does not shy away from us, but instead enters in to the middle of it all. May these testimonies bear witness to that truth and bring you the hope that does not disappoint.

These stories, and your own, matter. Let these pages remind you that even here, even now, hope lives on.

Sincerely,

Brian Dixon
Publisher, hope*books

About the Chapters

In Chapter 1, **Robin Heim** tells the story of a high-functioning single mother whose hidden trauma and overwhelming stress culminate in a severe depressive breakdown and psychiatric hospitalization. Beneath her capable exterior lay decades of unresolved abuse, loss, poverty, and suppressed grief that finally surfaced in therapy, where speaking her pain aloud became the beginning of healing. Through faith, self-awareness, community, and honest reflection, she comes to understand that depression is not weakness but the body and soul demanding care. Like kintsugi—where broken pottery is mended with gold—God gathers her shattered pieces and restores her into someone stronger, aware, and beautifully redeemed.

In Chapter 2, **Laurie Knudsen** recounts her journey through years of sexual abuse by her father, the crushing silence and shame she carried, and her struggle to believe God was present in her suffering. Though fear, guilt, and anger often eclipsed her faith, small sparks of hope—through prayer, a film hotline, trusted adults, and finally her mother's belief—became lifelines that led her to safety. Wrestling with injustice and forgiveness, she ultimately discovers that God had not abandoned her but was carrying her through the darkest seasons. Her story becomes a testimony that even in profound trauma, hope can be rekindled, healing is possible, and God's plans still hold a future beyond the pain.

In her chapter, author **Laura Lee Pettit** reflects on how God, the Master Gardener, revives dreams that once felt buried beneath fear, disappointment, and self-doubt. Through childhood memories of storytelling and worship, seasons of anxiety and striving, and one small act of courage—"clicking register"—she begins to see how God had been tending the soil of her heart all along. As faith is rekindled and long-dormant passions for writing and singing are restored, she discovers that no seed God plants is ever wasted. Ultimately, the chapter is an invitation to trust God's timing, take one faithful step forward, and believe that He still brings life to what we thought was lost.

In the fourth chapter, **Kristi May** shares her journey through insomnia, psychosis, divorce, and deep emotional despair, when hope felt distant and her future uncertain. In the midst of suffering, God met her through Scripture and a powerful, unmistakable confirmation in a park that reminded her she was seen, loved, and not forgotten. Though her healing did not restore everything she lost, it transformed her heart, renewed her mind, and rebuilt her life in ways she never expected. Ultimately, her story testifies that true hope is anchored in God alone—and that no one is too damaged, too broken, or too far gone to be healed, restored, and used for His glory.

In Chapter 5, **Elizabeth Bass** recounts the devastating loss of her beloved mother to cancer, the anger and grief compounded by medical neglect and broken promises surrounding her ashes, and the cascade of trauma that followed in the years after her death. From a collapsing body and hurried marriage to postpartum depression and decades of hardship, unresolved sorrow smoldered like a fire that would not go out. Yet over time, God gently transformed bitterness into peace, helping her see mercy even in painful details and beauty rising from ashes. Ultimately, the chapter reflects on the seasons of life and death, affirming that in God's hands, even the deepest grief can be redeemed in its time.

In her chapter, **Elaine Lopez** recounts the traumatic moment at eight years old when a trusted older boy lured her into abuse, shattering her innocence and exposing the devastating reality of hidden hypocrisy within her church community. After bravely escaping and speaking out, her life was forever marked by the pain and confusion of that violation. Yet through Scripture, prayer, trauma-informed healing, and the truth of God's Word, she begins to separate her identity from the trauma inflicted upon her. Anchored in Isaiah 43:1, the chapter declares that she is not defined by abuse but redeemed, called by name, and claimed by a just and healing God who restores what was broken.

In Chapter 7, **AnnaGrace Head** shares her journey from self-reliant striving to surrendered dependence as a wife and stepmother navigating grief, barrenness, and the pressures of blending a family. Having long tied her worth to performance and control, she finds herself exhausted and imprisoned by perfectionism, despite knowing the truths of grace. Through Scripture, suffering, and the gentle unraveling of her autonomy, God invites her to embrace weakness as the very place where His strength is made perfect. Ultimately, the chapter is a tender call to lay down striving, release control, and discover the freedom, intimacy, and renewal that come from resting fully in Christ's sufficient grace.

In her chapter, **Rita Dunham** recounts her journey through the devastating loss of her husband, the crushing weight of single motherhood, betrayal, and financial ruin. Faced with exploitation and heartbreak, she chose mercy over revenge, trusting God even when justice seemed within reach. Through seasons of loneliness, false friendship, and deep spiritual questioning, she discovered that God's grace truly is sufficient in weakness. Ultimately, her story is one of divine restoration—where loss gave way to purpose, faith deepened through suffering, and God rebuilt what was broken into something greater than before.

Chapter 1

Kintsugi in the Potter's Hands: Mending a Broken & Tender Spirit

by Robin Heim

"THE SPIRIT OF A MAN WILL SUSTAIN HIM IN SICKNESS, BUT WHO CAN BEAR A BROKEN SPIRIT?"

PROVERBS 18:14 (NKJV)

Friday—Day 1

I am thirty years old. I wake up early every day, on time. I go to the gym on my way to work. I style my hair, apply make-up, polish my nails, spritz on perfume, and dress for the day. I engage and have conversations with people. I am witty with a side of sarcasm. I smile.

I work two jobs: one as a full-time bank teller and the other as a part-time telemarketer. I attend the local community college. A single mother raising four daughters. I rent rooms in the home of a friend's mother and contribute to the food costs in a shared kitchen. Occasionally, I go out with friends. I am dating. Busy; busy trying to be a responsible mother, a dependable renter, a serious student, an understanding ex-wife, a good person. I am not consciously trying to diet, but I forget to eat a lot. I drink coffee all morning, and go without lunch because I forget to bring something, and can't afford to buy anything. Most evenings, I am too exhausted to eat when I come home.

My menstruation has stopped.

My mind feels as if it is imploding.

Today is my twin daughters' twelfth birthday. I have five dollars in my purse to spend on their gifts. I buy two pairs of colorful leggings from a popular discount clothing shop on my way home from work. I walk in the house, greet everyone, "Happy Birthday! I'll be right back," then walk down the hallway to my room. I close the door, slide down onto the floor, and start to wrap the gifts. As I wrap, I begin to weep. I cry through the wrapping of the presents. I finish, wipe my eyes, open the bedroom door, and walk down the hall towards the kitchen. We sing, "Happy Birthday," to my twins. I can feel the tears begin to pool on my lower eyelids. I let everyone know that I am tired and need sleep. I kiss all my daughters goodnight and then go back to my bedroom. Huge, heavy drops are pouring down my cheeks. I put on my pajamas and lay down across the bed. I cry myself to sleep. I cry through my sleep.

Saturday—Day 2

And I cry through my waking the next morning. And I cry on my way to my second job. I think I am ill. The flu, perhaps? At work, I continue to cry as I attempt to speak to the person I have called to ask if they are interested in an extended warranty on their appliance. My body wants to collapse and slide off the chair onto the floor. I muster enough strength to walk across the room to inform my supervisor that I am not feeling well, "I must have the flu." All this time, I have been crying. Big, heavy drops. I find my way to the parking lot, fall into the driver's seat, and procedural memory takes over. I cry on the way to the clinic. And I cry as I approach the admitting counter and inform the assistant that I am not feeling well.

This little light of mine goes out.

On a gurney in the emergency room—I open my eyes, still crying—the doctor hovers above me, my friend and her mother are standing behind him. "She is suffering from severe depression," he says.

"I can't be depressed. Don't tell my girls that. Don't tell Ernie." I plead.

I am angry. I am confused. I am scared.

Depression is a foreign visitor I don't want to entertain. It is the stranger I don't want my girls to meet. Ernie is the man I am in love with, but our relationship is not on solid ground yet. Thoughts, random and concrete, are filling my head as quickly as the tears are falling.

"We are going to have to keep her here for now, so we can assess her health and determine what the next best move is to help her heal," says the doctor.

The orderly comes in and gently transfers me from the gurney to the wheelchair. They are wheeling me to the resident psych-unit. My words are directed to everyone and to no one, "I can't stay here. I have to go home. I have children. I have to go to work on Monday." Raised voice now quieting, whimpering, whispering, mute.

My room opens onto a courtyard that separates the units from the lounge and dining area. Sitting in a hospital gown on the side of the bed, I look out through the open door onto the courtyard. My mind is in chaos, my heart is heavy, my soul is confused. How long have I been here?

"God, I don't understand. Why is this happening to me?"

It is then that I see Ernie walking across the courtyard toward me. He sits down on the bed and hugs me.

"I know you've told me that you've been struggling with your bills, your ex-husband, with many things. I've been an ass. I wasn't really listening. I'm sorry. Don't worry about the girls. Don't worry about anything. I'm going to speak to Father Phil and have him come here to see you. Just work on getting better." He leaves. Tears remain.

Sunday—Day 3

I rise and go to the dining area. As I eat, I watch the other patients. Many talk out loud, voices crisscrossing the area with no intended recipient. Others fuss over imaginary items on walls, on tables, in the space around them.

I don't belong here.

Ernie arrives around noon with Father Phil. We talk. I am prayed over. A nurse lets me know that it is time to see the hospital psychologist. I enter the office, sit down, and the session begins. "You've experienced an emotional breakdown. Tomorrow we are taking you across town to

Charter Oak. I believe it's a better facility for working on your recovery. You will meet with the psychiatrist once a day and attend group therapy daily. Your insurance will cover everything."

"Thank you," I say. Then I throw up.

God draws near to the broken in spirit. "…a broken spirit dries the bones" (Proverbs 17:22, NKJV). Emptiness itself takes up space and makes you feel full. Air is invisible, but fill a balloon with too much and it pops. Have you felt it, my friend? The brittle emptiness of despair as it fills your lungs to bursting, cracking bones and piercing skin? It is here, in your Garden of Gethsemane, where He kneels beside you. He's always known this day was coming.

Monday—Day 4

At Charter Oak, the resident psychiatrist admits me. I am given a toiletry pack with *no sharp objects* and assigned a room. One of the few items I am allowed to keep with me are photos of my daughters. I place them on the night-stand next to the twin bed; a gentle reminder of the good that is still in my life and why I need to take care of me— for them.

I call home and speak to my friend and her mother. They tell me not to worry about the girls; they will care for them. I want to speak to my girls, but they are not yet home from school, and I am not sure they will understand. I'm not crazy. I'm just…emotionally broken. Later in the evening, I call again and talk to my daughters. All I can bring myself to say is that I am okay and not to worry. I will be home soon.

Entering the lounge, patients are playing board games and watching television. The tears have stopped; my eyes sting from the sudden dryness. A nurse comes by on her evening rounds. She is pushing a cart filled with small, white paper cups. She rolls it over to me. Lifting a cup from the cart, she hands it to me with water. "What are these?" I ask her.

Pointing to each pill individually, she replies, "This one is to help you sleep, and this one is an antidepressant."

"No, thank you," I say.

She looks surprised. Everyone in the room looks at me in bewilderment.

"Are you sure you don't want them?" she asks.

"Yes, I am. How can I know I'm getting better if I'm medicated? When I can sleep soundly through the night, I'll know that I'm getting better."

For years, when I would share this part of my life with close friends, they would remark on how strong I had been to refuse medication. What they wouldn't tell me was that they had taken, or were taking, medication for their own bouts of depression or anxiety. I would find out much later in our friendships that they were afraid I might think less of them for doing so.

I've always avoided excessive drinking. I've also shunned any form of addictive medication. However, over the last four decades, there have been times when I have been prescribed medication for anxiety. Life happens—and if we believe that, "To everything there is a season, a time for every purpose under heaven" (Ecclesiastes 3:1, NKJV), then we must also acknowledge that God has provided physicians and medication with the purpose of helping us here, on earth, as part of His divine plan.

Tuesday—Day 5

I meet with the psychiatrist, it's difficult to hear him speak about me, my condition—I've stopped crying and feel okay now. Survival skills. We all have them. I have them. I had had a bad day, that's all. There are others in the world far worse off than I am. Right?

After the session, the psychiatrist shows me to the door and motions down the hall to the right, "The door to the left is where your group therapy is meeting. You will go directly to the group therapy session following our meetings every day."

The group consists of about twenty other patients and a counselor, their chairs pulled into a circle. Sitting down, I listen to their words. Stories laced with drug and alcohol addiction mostly. I can't relate. When it's my turn to speak, there just isn't much to say. After all, I've been handling my life. I'm not an addict. I hold a job. I'm responsible. I don't have issues like the rest of the group. Or so I think.

When I'm not in session with the psychiatrist or in group therapy, I walk around the grounds in my Michigan Wolverines sweatshirt, jeans, and high-top tennis shoes. I attend crafts and make coffee mugs. I play basketball or volleyball with other patients in the gym. I go to the dining hall to eat my meals alone. Or so I think, again.

Week Two

I notice that every time I walk to the dining hall, I am followed by a nurse or an orderly. They sit quietly at another table near me, observing. I mention this to another patient, and she explains, "They are monitoring your eating pattern."

"Why?" I ask.

"They probably think you have an eating disorder," she says.

At 5'5, I am 105 pounds, size 1. Eventually, the staff concludes that I do not have an eating disorder. Without rushing from one job to the next, and then to classes at college, I remember to eat.

I decide to nickname Charter Oak "Club Med." Being here is the closest to being on a vacation I could never afford: my bed is made for me each morning, I watch TV, play board games, go to the gym every day, participate in crafts, and eat, really eat, three meals prepared for me every day. Seeing the psychiatrist and attending group therapy sessions is my work.

One day, a patient asks the counselor why I am here. "She talks like she's a doctor," he says. "Not a patient like the rest of us." I'm here, listening to your stories, expressing my thoughts, isn't that what I'm supposed to do?

Each room at Club Med has its own shower, shared by two roommates. I am showering when I notice something on the top of the door frame across from the shower. When I am done, I exit the shower, grab the towel, and reach up to retrieve the item. It is a white, plastic, serrated knife from the dining hall. After I dry off and get dressed, I walk down to the nurses' station, hand one of them the knife, state where I found it and that I have no idea how it ended up there. That is when I am informed that the woman bunking next to me, who is always talking about her job at General Dynamics and her children, is suicidal and a repeat patient.

We, humans, are cunning animals. We are good at easing into new routines, avoiding all the warning signs that forced us to change direction. As John wrote, "However, when He, the Spirit of truth, has come, He will guide you into all truth..." (John 16:13, NKJV). Jesus is both our Revealer and Redeemer. Together with the Holy Spirit, He will shed light on the sorrow that consumes your heart, guide you through the self-reflection needed to identify the cause, and empower you with the strength to follow the way towards recovery.

Week Four

According to Bessel van der Kolk, M.D., *The Body Keeps the Score*, "The imprints of traumatic experiences are organized not as coherent logical narratives but in fragmented sensory and emotional traces."[1] Today was a day like all the rest in Group Therapy. Until it wasn't. Who is talking? Someone in the group is talking about their father, and now someone is crying. Sobbing. Wailing. Where is that deep, guttural sound coming from? Me. It's coming from me.

The wall I have built so carefully around me is cracking wide open. All the things I have so neatly piled up inside are spilling out willy-nilly, everywhere. All over my body. All over my chair. All over the floor around me. Words are spewing into the air. Some hang there. Some fall hard. No drugs. No alcohol. Just pain. Pain finally found a way out. Pain is my common denominator with everyone sitting here.

In the book of Lamentations, we are told to "...pour out your heart like water before the face of the Lord" (Lamentations 2:19, NKJV). Everything. Everything is spilling out over my lips.

Parents divorcing. Was I three? Molested by stepfather. Abandoned by mother. Going to live with my father. Alcoholic stepmother. Violent alcoholic. Father's death. He is just thirty-nine; I am just fourteen. No living trust. Stepmother inheriting the entire estate. In May 1970, Michigan law dictates that, if no Will, all goes to the surviving spouse.

Trying to escape her alcoholic rage. Her pinning me into a corner. Knee to my pelvis. Pushing me down. Grabbing my hair. Pounding my head into the floor, over and over. Lifting my face. Ripping an earring from my earlobe. Blood dripping down my neck. Screaming, "He died because of you! He didn't want to live long enough to raise a teenager!" Note on table the next morning, "I don't want you here when I get home."

Walking to the convent. Sister Mary Crispin greeting me. Throwing her arms around my shoulders. Walking me to the police department. Staying with me as I speak with the detective. The detective contacting my stepmother. Deciding that he didn't want to take me back home.

January 1971 in Detroit. Where to take a teen who isn't the problem? Safe houses for children didn't exist. The only place available was juvenile hall. Checked in. My life placed into a plastic bag, tagged, and shelved. Stripped and sprayed down with water. Handed clothing and a mattress. No sheets. No pillow. Overcrowded. Dragging the mattress into the hallway with dozens of other girls.

Next day, breakfast. Milk. Cereal. Hard-boiled egg. All snatched off the tray before I could find a seat. Only cold, unbuttered toast left.

Preliminary hearing. The judge releases me back to her custody. One condition—she doesn't drink. Clearly, the judge didn't understand alcoholism. Maybe it's because she's a woman. She can't be THAT bad?

Back to school. ONE teacher suspects. He asks me to wait after class. "Are you okay?"

I answer, "I'm fine."

Running away to California. To my paternal grandmother, the only blood relative I know. I've seen her three times in my fifteen years. A stranger, really.

Pregnant at 16. Boyfriend drives me to and from the abortion clinic. Then finds a new girlfriend.

Working at 17 as a waitress. New relationship. Living together. Pregnant. He doesn't want a baby—right now. Abortion, again. Too afraid to be totally on my own, so I stay. Getting married five months later. Pregnant again. Twins at 18. I uncover secrets surrounding his military discharge. Back and forth; together, not together. Separation. Divorce.

Three years later. Another relationship. Living together. A miscarriage. Two more babies. Deciding to get married. He's unfaithful—twice. Separation. Divorce, again.

A gay relationship, of sorts. Because...why not? Short, but long enough for me to realize that, regardless of gender, I am not good at choosing partners.

Three decades of trauma and loss; save only the blessing of four daughters.

Going to the welfare office. Seeking supplemental financial help. The social worker must assume I am receiving child support as part of my overall income, though neither ex-husband has paid any.

"Do you really think if I had $400 extra a month, I would be here?" The final answer— (on paper) I am $9 above the maximum cutoff limit for wages to qualify as low income, even for a family of five. So, I'm only eligible to receive $6 a month in food stamps. Thanks, but no thanks.

I'm not sure how much air I sucked out of the room and filled with my words. But I am sure of this. THIS is exactly how pain, in words spoken out loud, collides with the silence carried long and deep. Sucking it all up and shoving it all down, until your soul suddenly SCREAMS.

I'm a good person. I'm an honest person. If God does everything for a reason, I'm starting to wonder what the reason for all of this is. Why has my whole life been so damn hard?

I wasn't strong. I wasn't weak. I wasn't faithless. I wasn't faith-filled. I wasn't promiscuous. I wasn't bad, but I wasn't as good as I wanted to be. I was untethered. And I was angry.

The adult me knew better, but the teenage me lay beneath the rubble, raging at the father who died and left me alone. Alone with a stepmother whose addiction and pain I was far too young to understand or handle. Alone with those who would take everything he worked so hard for away from his only child. Alone to navigate the fall from an upper-middle-class life to near poverty. Struggling. Knowing there was a better way to live, confused as to how to obtain it. Exhausted in spirit and flesh. I loved him dearly; missed him incredibly.

And I knew. I knew now, as a parent, as a mother, that he never dreamed he would go so soon. That he thought he had time. Time to get everything in order, so I wouldn't be without. Time to show me the ropes. Time for him was not to be. I wept for the time we needed and didn't get. I wept for the grandchildren he would never hold. I wept for his voice that I couldn't hear anymore. And, finally, I let go of the anger.

And there. There, emptied of every word, the healing began.

The Kintsugi Master, with infinite wisdom and patience, gathers every piece and begins to seam my broken self into a stronger, more beautiful me.

As Lysa TerKeurst shares in her book, *Forgiving What You Can't Forget*, "My pain…needed to be verbalized—spoken out loud, acknowledged, recognized as real—and brought out into the light…to see myself as Jesus sees me—broken but still chosen."[2] Remember when women used to share information with each other regarding their sorrows and joys? Growing up in Detroit, my neighborhood was not only diverse, but it was filled with women who came from the "old country": Poland, Czechoslovakia, Persia (now known as Iran), Germany, and England. And they talked.

They talked about their health. They talked about church. They talked about marriage and children, life and death. Sharing allowed information needed for personal growth, problem-solving, and social bonding. It was the village we needed and seemingly lost overnight.

Instead of talking outwardly, we began to move inward, isolated and disconnected from each other and God. We started to think and behave the way we thought we should. Adopting an "I don't need any help" and "What happens in the house stays in the house" mindset. When was the last time you sat with a woman friend or neighbor and shared life? Not just the good and happy parts, but the ugly, brutal moments, too.

When I returned to my room, I found out that my roommate was in ICU—attempted suicide. I did not see her again for the remainder of my stay.

Week Six

I was eating regularly, sleeping soundly, and generally feeling better. Time to leave. Check, please!

I was told that menstruation had stopped because I had no body fat left, and my reproductive system was shutting down. My body had to warn me that I was too thin to sustain my life, because my mind was too busy trying to fix it by itself.

The Unbearable Lightness of Depression

"Now hope does not disappoint, because the love of God has been poured out in our hearts by the Holy Spirit who was given to us" (Romans 5:5, NKJV).

It isn't easy for relatives, friends, coworkers, or yourself to recognize depression. Severe, high-functioning depression, what I suffered from, is even harder to identify. Outwardly, I appeared to be managing my daily life between work, college, family, and other relationships. Mentally, I was able to mask my physical symptoms by thriving at work and school, maintaining social connections, ignoring what I needed (and didn't have), and smiling.

Depression isn't necessarily about being unhappy. I certainly wasn't unhappy. I was, however, overwhelmed and traumatized by circumstances and situations.

The concept that an event can only be considered traumatic if it occurs outside the range of ordinary human experiences is limiting. Circumstances connected to women experiencing abuse of any kind, divorce, or job loss, and the survival skills they implement, although starting to be recognized by mental health experts, still beg further examination.

The correlation between severe stress, or anxiety, and Post Traumatic Stress Disorder (PTSD) is beginning to emerge as psychologists study the changes that occur when women attempt to respond and adapt to stress or violence that continually disrupts the normal balance of life.

Women's rising resistance and subsequent exhaustion, during and immediately following incidents that produce extreme stress, often result in repression and avoidance as they attempt to recover and move forward.

When a woman is subjected to continual physical and mental pressure from an outside source, over time, stress creates a subconscious shift that overrides any fear concerning the situation, creating a feeling of control. This shift in thinking enables the woman to function through the ongoing trauma. How long, then, must the trauma reside, following the event, before the survivor is able to comprehend and articulate in words the full impact of their experience?

Despite the long history of PTSD, failure to equate post-traumatic stress as a disorder, along with the depression that accompanies it, as affecting women, perhaps, was due to the symptoms primarily being attributed to male military personnel following historically horrific events. Initially labeled "Shell Shock," medical experts noted that the effects of brutality and uncertainty on the battlefield lingered and affected soldiers far longer after they returned home.[3]

As female abuse complaints increased and became more complicated in the mid-1970's, scientists and health care workers began to reevaluate the effects of sexism and sex role stereotypes on women's health. While psychological theories increased, many of the theories still held on to primitive and biased myths regarding gender, continuing to view women's physical or neurological symptoms as being a form of hysteria or purely psychosomatic.

Eventually, a growing acknowledgement of the prevalence of violence in the lives of women, as well as an evolving clinical understanding of post-traumatic syndromes, began to challenge traditional psychiatric perspectives by asking how and why women are perceived differently from men in the mental health system.

Increased sensitivity and knowledge of how repeated or continued physical, sexual, mental, or emotional abuse affected women resulted in the diagnosis and treatment of trauma-related symptoms that were being presented outside the realm of military engagement, in everyday situations and circumstances found at home and at work.

According to Elizabeth Warren and Amelia Warren Tyagi, *The Two-Income Trap: Why Middle-Class Mothers and Fathers Are Going Broke*, "Most mothers tumbled down the economic ladder after they [divorced and] the drop [was] hardest for women in the middle and upper classes, since they [had] farther to fall."[4] The effect of overwhelming, traumatic situations and circumstances became evident as to the effect they had on the emotional, mental, and physical well-being of women.

The consequence of invalidation of self and self-knowledge from events like the death of a loved one, the dissolution of a marriage, chronic illness, and situational poverty following divorce or job loss often manifests in defenses like repression, silence, and dissociation.

In the United States, where the dominant myth is that an American, especially a middle- to upper-class citizen, should be able to pull themselves up by their bootstraps and rise above every adversity, the shame most women harbor not only exacerbates stress and trauma, but prolongs it, creating a natural refusal to seek medical or psychological help (Heim).

As van der Kolk states in his book, *The Body Keeps The Score*, "At the core of recovery is self-awareness [...] Becoming aware [is] how your body organizes particular emotions or memories [and] releasing sensations and impulses you once blocked, in order to survive." Be kind to yourself. Be aware of the season of life you are in and the ways that your body is responding. Take the time to take care of yourself, not only by making regular appointments to consult with a physician, but also by participating in activities that aid in relaxation and self-awareness. Life is hard, but God is good—and you deserve all the good He has in store for you.

Take Care of You

Read: Actively read—underscore, highlight, make notes in the margins. Informational books help you to recognize changes in yourself and to understand what may be happening. Seasonal and spiritual books help to quiet your soul. Fiction can sometimes help you to recognize yourself in the greater human experience. Here are a few recommendations for each.

The Body Keeps The Score: Brain, Mind, and Body In the Healing Of Trauma, Bessel van der Kolk, M.D.

Inner Gardening: Four Seasons of Cultivating the Soul and Spirit, Diane Dreher

The Cloister Walk, Katherine Norris

Hello Beautiful, Ann Napolitano

Listen: To music and podcasts. Here are a few of my favorites.

<u>Music</u>

"A Midwinter Night's Dream," Loreena McKennitt

"My One and Only Thrill," Melody Gardot

"The Memory of Trees," Enya

"Winter into Spring," George Winston

Podcasts

Struggling Well with Tandem Spirituality

The One You Feed with Eric Zimmer

Everything Happens with Kate Bowler

Remind{her} with Julianne Clapton

Write Letters: When was the last time you sat down and wrote a letter to a friend? There is no better way to be in the present and practice mindfulness than to take pen to paper and share your thoughts with someone. Colorful or seasonal stationery, colored pens, and a collection of stamps can lift your spirit. It's an awesome feeling to receive a reciprocating letter in response, but be open to those who respond with a phone call, email, or text.

Keep a Health Journal: Keep track of your body and mind. List your doctor visits and what was shared. How are you feeling? Include quotes or articles you come across that speak to you and your health.

Stay Active: Repetition reduces anxiety. Knitting, crocheting, embroidering, drawing, painting – keep your hands in motion to ease and organize your thoughts. Walk, jog, or run, practice Yoga, Tai Chi, or meditation—address both body and mind to build endurance both physically and mentally.

Engage: Gather people close to you and share, openly and authentically. Ask for medical or psychological help, without shame, embarrassment, or judgment.

United Way (https://www.unitedway.org) is a great place to start. They can find counseling in your area, including any that charge on a sliding scale.

Pray: Prayers don't have to be long to be effective. "Help me" is a complete sentence, and God hears two words just as easily and swiftly as a full paragraph or litany.

Forgive: When I think of *Forgiving What You Can't Forget*, I am reminded of the words Lysa TerKeurst said as she struggled to forgive those who hurt her, "I forgive [insert name]. And whatever my feelings don't yet allow for, the blood of Jesus will surely cover." Forgiving has been easier as the years fall away—but forgetting hasn't always been sustainable as moments arise, and I'm flooded with stinging feelings of betrayal or sorrow. So, when this happens to you, as it has to me, remember that His blood was shed for [insert name] just as surely as it was for you.

Finding Hope in the Darkness: Learning That God Is There Even When We Think He's Not

by Laurie Knudsen

I can still feel the ice-cold water pouring down on me as I sat on the floor of the shower, knees to my chest, sobbing. I was confused and scared, and I had no idea what might happen moving forward. All I did know was that it must be my fault. It was my fault that I had forgotten all the things he had done to me, and now I was willingly moving in with my former abuser, my father. What had I done? I was 16 years old, naively hoping for something better, suddenly realizing I had walked back into the pit.

I lived in fear and without hope for most of my childhood. My father was an alcoholic with a quick temper. My earliest memories of him are those of corporal punishment. I was terrified of him and did my best to be good at all costs, never wanting to upset him.

My life changed even more drastically in the summer I turned 12. My parents announced to my 10-year-old brother and me that my mom, who had just gone to work for the first time in my life, was going to have a baby.

My thoughts were ubiquitous. I wanted to be excited about a new brother or sister, but I was immediately in fear of what might happen if that baby made my father angry.

So why would I be excited about a new sibling? All I could think about was how I would have to protect this innocent child.

Just days after their announcement, my mom was at work, and my brother was upstairs taking a nap. I had made lunch for him and my father, and was clearing the dishes when my father started helping me. This was odd because he was from the generation that did not believe that doing dishes was a man's job.

I was at the kitchen sink when he came up behind me and began touching me in a manner a man should never touch a child, let alone his own daughter. I was frozen in a new sort of fear, with no idea what was happening or why. He led me to the bathroom, where the touching continued. I was so confused as he guided my hand to the places he wanted it to be. When it was over, he left me standing there and went to take a short nap himself before waking my brother.

I was unable to contain the flood of tears. My childhood innocence was destroyed, stolen from me, along with all hope of what could happen next.

This was a normal lunchtime occurrence as the summer continued. I would often escape to the stairway that led to the upstairs bedrooms. This is where I would sob and, in my continued astonishment, try to acknowledge what was happening to me.

My brother found me crying one day and wanted to know what was wrong. I told him nothing as I brushed the tears off my face. He continued to ask, and I continued to say it was nothing, disturbed by his questioning.

He wouldn't take no for an answer and threatened to say something to our mom, so I told him. I told my little brother what our father had been doing to me. He called me a liar and said that was a terrible thing to say. He told me he was going to tell Mom that I was lying and saying terrible things. He never did; he either simply forgot or buried my horrible truth.

That was when I knew, *if my own brother didn't believe me, who would?*

As the summer continued, my mom began experiencing complications with her pregnancy and had to be rushed to the hospital. While there, she had emergency surgery for what ended up being an ectopic pregnancy that nearly took her life.

A Cry for Hope

We didn't go to church much, mostly on holidays, but I did know about God and Jesus thanks to my maternal grandmother. I was even able to attend a church camp in the summer when I turned 11, and that was when I gave my heart to the Lord.

When I visited my grandparents, my grandpa would play the guitar, and they would both sing, teaching me beautiful hymns. My grandmother was a prayer warrior, always talking to God. So, on the night that I thought my mom might die, I tried talking to God myself. I was terrified of being alone with my father on a permanent basis. He had told me that because of her pregnancy, there were things she couldn't do, so I would have to. I was even more terrified of what that might mean if she were gone.

So, I ask you, dear reader, has there ever been a time in your life when you felt lost and alone? Unheard, or perhaps afraid to be heard? I know what that feels like all too well, and I am here to tell you that even when we have more doubt than we can carry, there is one thing we can do, even if it is while sobbing, even if we can hardly utter the words we need to say...we can cry out to Him, if only for comfort in the moment.

I can still see myself lying on the living room floor, where my father had left me. He had come in after work, molesting me before going to the hospital to see my mom. He told me how she had lost a lot of blood and would need to have surgery.

So right there, I did the only thing I had left to do: I prayed. Out loud, through heavy sobs, I asked the God I wanted to know more to help me. I begged and pleaded for my mom to be OK, that He would not leave me alone with my father. I didn't know at the time, but that prayer was my first connection to hope.

The dictionary defines hope as "a feeling of expectation and desire for a certain thing to happen."[1] On that dark and lonely night, hope was all I had to cling to. And the only way of keeping it was to cry out to the only One who would be able to give it to me.

Hope As a Sustainer

My mom would come home after a few days; she explained that she was OK, but she lost the baby. In my young mind, I immediately believed that it was my fault that the baby died. I had been selfish in my prayer, only praying for my mom and to save myself; so, because I didn't pray for the baby, it died.

It would be years before I could let go of the burdensome guilt I placed on myself and grab hold of the metaphoric candle, its light barely flickering, of hope.

So, I ask yet another question of you, dear reader. In the moments that seem the darkest, are you able to reach out and grasp hold of that barely lit candle and know that there is more? That He, our loving God, has more for you, especially in the darkest times. Once we have invited Him in, we are never alone, never without hope.

I want you to close your eyes and imagine the footprints in the sand. Take in a few deep breaths and release all that is negative and overwhelming. With each breath, I want you to look ahead, on the horizon, to the shape that is walking, the One leaving those footprints as you trail behind.

Do you see Him? Do you see His arms wrapped lovingly around someone? Look closer, dear friend; that someone He *chooses* to carry is you. Those are *His* footprints, not your own, and He has gladly taken on your burdens and your secrets because of His unending love for you.

Mary Stevenson states at the end of the poignant poem, *Footprints in the Sand,* "During your times of trial and suffering, when you see only one set of footprints, it was then that I carried you."[2]

Once more, giving us another glimpse of possible hope. Yet, the abuse would continue sporadically over the next year, less frequently over time.

On my 14th birthday, my father told me he and my mom were getting divorced. I was so angry at them both. I couldn't understand why they would do that to our family. I moved into town with my mother. My brother chose to stay in the country with our father. I missed my brother because I only saw him on weekends now, but I adjusted to living in town with my mom.

My mom would remarry, adding two more kids to our family; suddenly, every other weekend, there would be these two extra kids who did not have to follow the same rules I did. My mom would say it was easier not to fight about the "little" things and that they were only there a few days out of the month. This fueled my anger at Mom because she had rules to follow, and my father did not.

At the end of my sophomore year and just before my 16th birthday, the fighting with my mom increased. When I was at my father's, he would say things that led me to believe life would be different and more fun if I came to live with him. He even promised me I could have my own car.

Hope in the Midst for Change

Hoping for something better, I moved in with my brother, father, and his girlfriend.

I thought the grass would be greener at my father's; besides, I missed my brother terribly and wanted to spend time with him again.

It would only be a few days before I was sobbing in that shower in disbelief. *Look what I've done to myself. How was I so stupid? How did I forget the countless times he had touched me before?* And now... now it was so much worse. My father was no longer only molesting me; now he was raping me.

Have you done this? Have you buried something so deep that it seemed to no longer exist? Then, when triggered, the wash of all the chaos and pain falls over you. What do you do?

Do you, like me, blame yourself? We should have known better. Did you believe that the choice you made was final, so that you couldn't take it back? I know I did, and I had little to no hope in those initial days. I had nothing more than a barely mustard-seed-sized hope in the midst of it all. I had no plan of what to do, other than survive. That survival would not be easy. There would never be a car for me to use. It was there, but in need of parts and repair.

It is in these difficult and sometimes scarring moments that we cannot give up hope. Because having hope amid our darkest trials is where the real magic happens. It often can't be seen at the time, but again, it is like seeing those footprints in the sand and grasping the significant understanding that we are not alone. Perhaps with this knowledge, the candle burns a little brighter, and our hope is easier to perceive. And fear will not win the war.

I was a 16-year-old girl constantly in fear of everything. Can you relate?

What fears or secrets hold you back from grasping hold of the hope that is there if you only look? Are you constantly crying in the dark, hiding from the danger that envelops you in the midst?

When the house was empty, and I was alone, I would curl up in the bathroom and lock the door. This is where I would do my homework, as it was much safer than my room. My bedroom was in an open basement without a door. I had a sheet for one of my walls. There was no lock to keep my father away from me; I was a hostage in my own home.

I had chosen to live with my father, so I had to deal with the consequences. I would just have to wait until I graduated and moved away, never to return. But as time moved along and the weeks became months, it was harder and harder to get through a given day. I was terrified of being alone. Because if I were alone with my father, there would be an unwanted encounter; I could count on it.

Have you ever made a decision that you feel you couldn't take back? Have you been trapped and controlled by someone and couldn't see a way out? Did you, or do you, feel that you just must "deal with the consequences" because you are broken and damaged, and no one will care? Is the hope in your life dwindling to near non-existence?

It doesn't have to stay that way. There is a way that is better, a way that is far from the darkness you feel smothered by. Because in the midst of the darkness, there is also hope. You must search for and find that flickering candle, that mustard seed of hope. Search for the One who loves you and is waiting for you to call out to Him and to simply be loved.

I attempted to escape my hell at home by getting involved in extracurricular activities at school. I ran cross-country and became very involved with our Speech & Drama team.

My first attempt to seek help, to reach out for that candle of hope, was when I wrote a speech about sexually abused children in daycare centers. The McMartin case from a center in California was all over the news; the children in their care were being molested by the caregivers. When I did my research, there were many comments and facts about the abuser generally being someone the child knows, including a family member, even the child's father.

The candle shone a little brighter when I read this, and I felt the strength to reach out for help. My coach and teacher had me remove that sentence because she felt it really didn't have anything to do with my speech. My cry for help went unnoticed.

Are you feeling unnoticed, dear friend? Do you think that no one sees? I understand, and it is possible we could shout our grievance from the rooftops, and it would fall on deaf ears, but there is One who always hears us, but like David, we have to cry out!

"How long, Lord? Will you forget me forever? How long will you hide your face from me? How long must I wrestle with my thoughts and day after day have sorrow in my heart? How long will my enemy triumph over me?" (Psalm 13:1–2, NIV).

I tried to talk to God. I tried to understand: if He loved me, then why, *WHY* was this happening to me? Why would he let my father do such horrible things to me?

The stress of my secret would cause me to end up in the hospital. After collapsing at school from terrible stomach pains that would be diagnosed as an ulcer, my father would stay at my bedside, portraying the caring father. I lied to the doctor about having sex. I told him I was a virgin. My father was in the chair beside me when I told this lie. He never said anything in exact words, but I thought maybe, just maybe, he had, in that moment, felt remorse.

Our junior class had a Slave Auction (where the participants do manual labor for an hourly cost) to raise money for prom; my father, who rarely attended any school activities, showed up. He wanted to "buy" me for a day of "helping" him. It was a terrible day, and I knew the abuse would never end, at least not until I left for college. It was at this time that I stopped talking to God. I quit asking for his protection because, in my heart, I thought He simply didn't care about me or the abuse I was enduring.

Hope Shines Bright

Shortly after I was hospitalized, there was a rare night when everyone was home. After dinner, we all sat together to watch the made-for-TV movie, *Something About Amelia*, with Ted Danson and Roxanne Zal, which depicted the story of a young teenage girl who was being molested by her father.[3]

I will never forget this film and how it helped to save my life as it was. It was difficult watching it in the same room as my father, my abuser. Holding back my tears was one of the most difficult things I have ever done.

I can still picture it as if it happened only yesterday. My brother and I are lying on the floor, heads propped up on our chins. My father was sitting in his chair, and his girlfriend was in hers. His girlfriend kept commenting on what she would do if someone did that to her child. Meanwhile, my father didn't say a word.

At the end of the movie, it provided an 800 number to call for help. I kept silently repeating it over and over because I couldn't write it down until later. I did finally get the number written down and hid it in a small box of crayons. I tried calling it once, but my father walked in, and I had to quickly hang up. But now, I finally knew that my voice deserved to be heard and, more importantly, that I wasn't as alone as I thought.

I was at my mom's house for the weekend; I had gotten home from the speech meet, which had not gone well. My mom and I were getting into yet another argument. She was very frustrated with me. She told me to get my stuff, and she would take me early because she was done fighting with me. I told her I wouldn't go because it wasn't time to go yet, and she couldn't make me go.

Have you been in what you considered a safe place and didn't want to leave it unless you absolutely had to?

I don't know what was different, but for the first time, she looked at me, r*eally looked at me,* and asked why I didn't want to go home. I lied and told her it was nothing and that she could do whatever. She kept pushing, asking me more questions. She asked if he was hitting me. I yelled, "NO, just drop it; take me home if that's what you want." She said she wouldn't take me anywhere if I didn't tell her what was really going on. I told her to forget it, because she wouldn't believe me anyway.

Is there someone you can trust who would believe you if you only spoke your truth?

The next thing she asked me was, "Does he make you have sex with him?" I simply nodded yes through my tears. I heard her blood-curdling scream, "No, not my baby!" By this time, my stepdad was in the room, asking what was happening. I still thought they were going to make me go back to my father's house. I can still hear myself crying, weeping, and begging them to please let me stay. My mother kept reassuring me I wasn't going anywhere.

I told my secret, and someone believed me.

Who can you talk to? Who can you share your deepest hurt with? Even if it is a hurt so carefully buried in the depths of your soul. The years, perhaps decades, do not matter; what matters is that you allow yourself to be seen and heard, even in the darkest of presentations.

The next few days were crazy, filled with an extensive interrogation with the police, as I had to tell them about every time my father ever touched me. I felt like this day would never come. Now, I just wanted it to end. It was so awkward telling the officer, even though she was a woman, all the horrid details from over the years.

Unfortunately, my father would get out on bond and then jump bail, leaving my healing and recovery in a weird sort of limbo until they finally found him months later.

From the very beginning, I always wanted to face him, to tell whoever wanted to listen what he had done to me. I wanted him to know I was no longer afraid of him.

Unfortunately, due to a legal issue having to do with his Miranda rights, I had to accept a plea bargain of one count. The man who abused me for close to a decade was going to be charged for only ONE time of molesting me! This made me angry again, angry at God because my father was not being properly punished.

Hope and Forgiveness Heal

At this time, I was working at the local grocery store. I worked a lot of nights with a young, new manager who helped me to begin to move forward in my life. I had some of the most difficult but most healing conversations with that manager after work. He allowed me to share my anger, my rage, and what I felt was so unjust, reminding me that God is the final judge and that He would redeem me for all my father had done to me. He reminded me to keep the faith and have hope.

Hope that can be found in the little things in my life, no matter how small. To look for the things that made me smile and hold on to those things, those moments. He also told me that if I didn't allow myself to forgive my father, I would never get out of the pit of darkness I was metaphorically living in. My flickering candle would be distinguished.

Once I was free from my father's abuse, I went through extensive counseling. Over time and with a lot of prayer, I came to the day when I could genuinely say, "I forgive my father." That forgiveness doesn't mean forgetting all he did and how broken he made me become. God loves and forgives me for my own poor choices; how could I not forgive others for their bad choices, too?

We can choose to give all our hurt, all our pain, and all our shame to the true Father. The Father who never left me alone, even when I thought I was. He didn't leave you alone either, dear friend. I have found comfort in knowing that God will continue to walk me through all the trials and tribulations of life. No matter how broken we may be. This is why I hold firm to my life verse from Jeremiah:

"'For I know the plans I have for you,' declares the Lord, 'plans to prosper you and not to harm you, plans to give you hope and a future'" (Jeremiah 29:11, NIV).

When we look back at difficult times in our lives, we can see where we may have tried to ignore God, but that doesn't mean He wasn't there doing the best He could to keep us safe from someone else's bad decisions. Remember all those moments when there was only one set of footprints in the sand? He was carrying me; He was carrying you, too.

As my emotional wounds have slowly healed, I knew that one day I would be strong enough to share my story so that I might be able to help others in their own healing journey. I share my story today, speaking my truth for anyone who wants to listen. I speak my truth to those who are feeling lost and are struggling with demons of their own. I know what it is like to carry the shame that a secret like this places on your heart, on your very soul.

So, remember, my dear friend, you are not alone. You too can share your secret, your truth. God will help you find someone who listens, who believes, and who will help you find true healing.

I would never have chosen the path I was given. I never wanted to be abused by my earthly father. That would have never been my plan; however, God, in His ultimate goodness and wisdom, did allow it to happen. He gave my father free will, and my father chose to walk outside of God's perfect will, which in turn caused horrible pain and suffering for me.

I know that God has always had a plan for me and my life, and if sharing my story helps one person, then I have done what I set out to do. My pain and suffering will not have been in vain. It is my hope that God can work through my story to help you work through your own, ultimately finding you hope in your future. God can prosper you and give you hope and a future, despite whatever you have gone through. I am a living testimony of that truth.

Finding Your Hope

Are you hurting or hiding due to something that was done to you? Is the pain and shame of the situation drowning you? There is something you can do. You can call out to the Father and ask Him to guide you, to lead you to a place of safety. Ask Him for His guidance and the courage to do the hard things.

Ask Him to place someone in your life that will be there just as unconditionally as He is. Find a church if you don't have one. Go and be present in His house; surround yourself with people who love Him and want to love you. Join a fellowship faith group, something small and simple, where you can feel safe. Share about yourself as you see fit, and as the relationships grow, you just might find the person you are meant to unburden yourself to and finally be free.

As I complete these thoughts God has given me to share with you, I am reminded of the third chapter of Ecclesiastes and the dark-light words that remind us that *everything* is indeed a gift from God. Its author is speaking of the many God-given blessings.

"There is a time for everything, a season for every activity under the heavens: a time to be born and a time to die... a time to kill and a time to heal, a time to tear down and a time to build, a time to weep and a time to laugh, a time to mourn and a time to dance... a time to tear and a time to mend, a time to be silent and a time to speak..." (Ecclesiastes 3:1–7, NIV)

It is time, dear friend, to heal; time to build something new in your life; a time to move from your weeping to laughing, to no longer mourn, but to dance; it is time to mend from all that has wounded you, and most importantly, the time for silence has ended, and it is time to speak your truth. He wants you to be heard.

So, align yourself where you can feel safe and loved. Be good to you. Take time for yourself, in prayer and meditation, or, as I have also found, writing and journaling to express the truths of your heart. I have ebbed and flowed over my healing journey, and it is my writing that provided me with the most peace, comfort, and the strength I needed in a given moment.

Meditation took effort and time, but once I took the time to try... I have found that when I am truly *still* and simply *listen*, He guides my thoughts and fills my heart with a comfort that only comes from Him. It is in those quiet and connected moments that I know without a doubt that He is God, my Father, my friend.

My final prayer for you is that these words will give you the courage you need to do what you might now consider impossible; that these words will allow you to feel the necessary hope that will grow and become a platform for you to stand on, a hope that will show you the way to peace on earth and the wonderful knowledge of what comes after. God is growing something good in me and also in you.

Chapter 3

The Master Gardener of Dreams: How God Revives What We Thought Was Lost

by Laura Lee Pettit

No way! I am not a fearful person. Or am I? Is it really okay to step into my dream?

The questions echoed in my heart as I sat at my kitchen table, journal open before me, the morning sunlight cutting through the blinds in slivers. I wanted to trust, but the memory of past failures clung like heavy vines around my heart. My chest tightened as doubts shadowed my thoughts, holding me captive, whispering lies I'd believed for years: *You're not good enough. Who do you think you are? Dreams like that aren't meant for you.*

I wanted to silence those thoughts. But instead, I sat with them as they swirled like smoke, darkening the hope that had been flickering in my heart.

More sunlight was slowly creeping across the table until it illuminated the words on my iPad screen. My finger hovered over a link in an email: "Register." I took a trembling breath and clicked.

That single click revived a dream I thought had long been buried. As that dream stirred, so did the memories of where it first began—long before adulthood, long before fear, long before I knew the Master Gardener pressed a seed of calling into my heart.

When I was six years old, my world shifted overnight. My family packed everything familiar and drove across the country from the Midwest to the West Coast. For a shy little girl who often felt unseen, it was a strange and unsettling new world. New streets. New faces. A new school, and I had no idea where I belonged.

Amid all that change, something small but steady met me where I was. In my first-grade classroom, my teacher began reading *Charlotte's Web* aloud each day. As her voice filled the room, the story wrapped around my lonely heart like a warm hug. Wilbur—the little pig who longed not for food, but for friendship and connection—became my companion in that new, uncertain place. His fear felt like mine. His longing echoed my own.

My teacher—though I didn't have words for it then— was the first "word gardener" in my life. She planted the seed of storytelling deep in my soul and watered it with her passion for books. She cultivated it with her gentle voice, her love of words, and her faith in a small girl who listened closely.

As a quiet, introverted child, I found safety and adventure between the pages of books. The words seemed alive; they moved and shimmered, inviting me in. They carried me to worlds where I wasn't afraid to be myself. The words on the page leapt out like tiny sparks, igniting something inside me that I didn't yet understand—but deeply felt.

Those sparks stirred my own imagination. They nudged me to grab a pencil and fill my own pages. My words were tentative, yet alive with possibility, fueled by wonder and curiosity. Something had been awakened, even if I could not yet see what it would become.

Over time, the world has a way of drying up creative soil. My words became hesitant, uncertain—like a seed trapped beneath drought-hardened ground, waiting for rain and struggling to surface. Self-doubt crept in, whispering lies: *You're not good enough. No one cares what you have to say.*

The seed remained underground, waiting.

Then came another "word gardener," my high school creative writing teacher whose encouragement spilled over my fragile lines. She poured life into my parched soil with her affirmation.

She saw beauty in what I wrote and urged me to keep writing. Under her care, that dormant seed broke through the ground. A tiny green bud stretched upward, hungry for light, growing toward the dream I barely dared to name. My dream began to sprout, busting through to become a bud, striving to grow, change, and show all the beauty that awaited inside the bud.

As the seasons of life unfolded—school, marriage, motherhood, career—the weeds of unbelief crept in to take root. My tender bud of a dream was smothered by insecurity and comparison. I looked at other people's success and thought, *Why bother? I'll never measure up.* The weight of "not enough" pressed down like layers of soil, and my budding dream disappeared beneath it. I repeated the lie so many dreamers whisper when life grows heavy: *It's too late.*

Still, even buried seeds are not dead.

The bud remained hidden beneath layers of fear, its beauty waiting to bloom. In that darkness, God's hand never stopped tending the soil.

Decades later, as I sat at my kitchen table, with the rays of the sun shining light on my screen, I clicked "Register," and something shifted. It was small, almost imperceptible—a single act of courage—but heaven must have smiled that day.

That simple act of obedience opened the door to a writer's garden full of grace-filled truth. A community of word gardeners who cultivated my long-forgotten bud of a dream. It was as if I had stepped into a new garden—a place where fellow writers tilled the soil of their dreams together. Slowly, the dirt shifted, the ground softened, the seed stirred once more, awakening the bud.

Each coaching call became a drop of living water, unkinking the hose tangled by fear and shame. Growth began again—small and steady. The hose of God's grace was flowing freely again.

Then came the moment I'll never forget. During a live coaching session, my words appeared on the screen. I became aware I was holding my breath as the coach acknowledged me by name. Instantaneously, tears welled up, blurring my vision as the words of my story—the ones I had hidden for so long – were spoken aloud. The minuscule sprout that was peeking out of the ground developed and flourished.

In that moment, I was seen. Not just by the coach or the community, but by the One who had planted the seed to begin with.

Through the season of cultivation, the writers' gardeners were instruments for the connection to the Master Gardener, who cuts, trims, and prunes to bring life. It was as if a twisted garden hose was straightened, and living water was soaking my dream into a plant.

God, the Master Gardener, had been tending my dream all along, coaxing life back into the soil of my soul.

As I poured myself into writing again, I discovered something deeper—my stories were not just *my* stories. They were *God's* stories. He was using them to heal my heart, to reveal His faithfulness, to encourage, and to speak hope to others.

He was reviving not just my dream—but me.

As my writing flourished again, another memory began to surface from the soil of my heart—a song from long ago.

When I was nine years old, my family didn't attend church regularly. We didn't pray together, read scripture, or talk about God. Faith was something distant—something that belonged to other people.

That year, our family began attending a small Lutheran church, so my youngest brother could be christened. I remained captivated by reading and especially drawn to the Bible stories in Sunday School. During December, the church children's choir was preparing for their Christmas program, and when I heard the announcement, something inside me leapt.

I loved to sing. I didn't know whether I had a good voice—I just knew that singing filled me with joy. The idea of singing at church for Christmas felt magical. I could hardly believe I would get to sing for Jesus at Christmas.

My parents even bought me a new dress for the occasion—something fancy, which was a rare luxury for our tight-budget family. I hung it proudly in my closet and counted the days with anticipation until the program, excitement building like a rocket waiting for liftoff.

When the time finally came, my body failed me, and everything unraveled.

I woke up feverish, my throat on fire, raw and swollen. The doctor's words confirmed what I feared—diagnosed with strep throat and tonsillitis. My neck was so inflamed that you could not see its definition.

My fancy new dress hung untouched as disappointment and tears streamed down my cheeks.

I remember lying in bed, imagining the other children in all their festive outfits and smiling faces, singing without me. The joy I had felt now seemed cruelly out of reach. I was crushed.

That evening, with a child's stubborn hope, I slipped on the dress anyway. Standing alone in our empty dining room, I sang softly to God through a hoarse, raspy voice. My body was weak, my voice faint—but my heart meant every word.

That was my first act of worship for God's gift of Jesus to the world.

And though I didn't know it then, heaven heard.

Life went on. Church faded from our family's rhythm; faith slipped quietly out of view, and so did my connection to God. I forgot that night. I forgot the little girl who sang through her grief and loss.

During the years that followed, I kept trying to recapture that early joy I once knew. The kind of joy that made my heart feel weightless, the kind that made singing to God seem as natural as breathing. Then life grew heavier, and disappointments settled where joy once lived. Slowly, that pure childlike faith faded beneath the weight of busyness, responsibility, and self-reliance. Consequences from choices I couldn't undo left a residue of regret.

By the time I reached adulthood, my life looked full and beautiful from the outside—a loving husband, a cherished daughter, and the semblance of a steady career. Yet inside, I was unraveling. Anxiety became a quiet companion that followed me into every role I tried to perform: wife, mother, daughter, sister, aunt, friend, employee. Some nights I would wake with my heart pounding so fiercely I thought it might burst. The only thing that seemed to steady the storm inside was the rhythmic motion of my rocking chair—the same chair where I had read bedtime stories to our little girl. As the chair creaked beneath me, my racing thoughts began to slow. The motion became my prayer, though I didn't yet know how to find the One who could truly calm the waves within me.

What I couldn't see then was that the Master Gardener had never left my side. Even when I neglected the soil of my soul, He was there—quietly protecting the dormant seeds He had planted long ago. Seeds of faith. Seeds of worship. Seeds of joy. I thought they had died, buried under years of striving, but they were only waiting for His touch to awaken them again.

Like an explorer searching for lost treasure, I began to dig. My search for peace led me down many paths, but ultimately, it was our curious, free-spirited daughter—her laughter, her wonder, her open-hearted joy—that led me home. She was about the same age I had been when I first wanted to sing for Jesus. I would watch her twirl and dance through our living room, singing without fear. It was as if Jesus Himself was whispering through her laughter, "This is what joy looks like when it's free".

After so many years of quiet ache and disappointment, through her eyes, I began to see again. I remembered the One who had placed the dream in my hands and the song in my heart.

It was through her that I encountered Jesus once more—not as a distant figure, but as a living presence inviting me to surrender. And that's exactly what I did. I made a decision of faith—a quiet but decisive "yes" to the One who had never stopped pursuing me. Jesus was the joy I had been missing, and writing was the tender shoot of a dream He had planted long ago.

"You will seek me and find me when you seek me with all your heart" (Jeremiah 29:13, ESV).

It took years for the truth of that verse to take root in my soul. Slowly, I came to understand how deeply God loved me—how fully He saw me, knew me, and delighted in me even when I felt unworthy. The same God who had once met me in my childhood wonder now met me in my weary adulthood.

I learned that there is no burden too heavy for God to lift, no heart too anxious for Him to calm. Sometimes His provision looks different from what we expect, but that doesn't mean He isn't working. Every season—the waiting ones, the restless ones, even the weary ones—become sacred when placed in His hands.

Because with God, nothing is ever wasted.

More than thirty years later, God tenderly brought that memory of my first act of worship back to my mind—not to reopen an old wound of hurt for what was lost, but to redeem it.

When my church announced auditions for the adult Christmas choir, something stirred in me again. That same childlike joy I felt as a little girl bubbled up, yet this time, it was deeper – rooted in gratitude. I joined, not knowing that God was orchestrating something deeper than music.

Standing there among a sea of voices worshipping in song, as the words flowed from my lips, I felt His presence wrap around me. The same God who had heard my small croaky song in an empty dining room was listening again—this time surrounded by the sound of a worshiping congregation, lifting praises to His name.

Overcome with emotion, tears welled up in my eyes as I realized—He had never forgotten.

He redeems even the smallest moments, turning childhood disappointment into adult joy.

That's what God does.

He resurrects the buried things.

He redeems what was broken and lost.

He breathes life into forgotten dreams.

The Master Gardener was not finished with me.

Psalm 135:6–7 (ESV) reminds us: "Whatever the Lord pleases, He does, in heaven and on earth, in the seas and all the deeps. He it is who makes the clouds rise at the end of the earth, who makes lightnings for the rain and brings forth the wind from His storehouses."

He is the Lord, the Master Gardener of all creation. He knows when to bring rain, when to let roots grow strong in silence, and when each seed is ready to sprout.

Jesus gives us this same picture in John 15:1, NIV, when He says, "I am the true vine, and my Father is the gardener." The Father tends, prunes, nurtures, and draws forth fruit—not out of pressure but out of love. Pruning can feel painful, but Jesus assures us it is so we may bear more fruit (John 15:2). And the fruit He desires is not merely productivity, but love—fruit that remains (John 15:16).

And Romans 11:36 (MSG) declares: "...Everything comes from Him; everything happens through Him; everything ends up in Him. Always glory! Always praise! Yes. Yes. Yes."

That includes *your* story and *mine*.

If the Master Creator's very words called galaxies into being, how could we not trust Him to bring forth beauty from our own small dreams? Surely His word can revive the dreams within us. The same God who tends vineyards and coaxes flowers from winter soil knows how to bring life out of us.

If we believe in Him, that means we are worthy and capable of realizing our blossoming dream. That we are made to come alive—designed and equipped to move into our heart's desire, to walk into the dreams He placed in our hearts long ago.

If He designed the delicately woven veins of a leaf and the rhythm of ocean tides, could He not also design our purpose?

If He can plan the intricate pattern of a snowflake, can He not also plan the details for our destiny?

The answer is yes. Always yes.

Where is He inviting you to take one small step toward the dream He planted in your heart?

Still, most of us don't simply glide into our God-given dreams. We wrestle. We question. We wonder if we are truly called. Fruit often forms in the very places where fear once took root.

Even now. I still wrestle between hope and fear. Between *What if I fail?* and *What if this is exactly what God made me for?*

And every time the fear starts to rise, God whispers the same truth He spoke through Isaiah 43:1 (ESV): "...Fear not, for I have redeemed you; I have called you by name, you are mine."

When I exhale the lies that I am not enough and inhale the truth that I am His, peace begins to take root again. God is still in the resurrection business. He is still calling His children to an abundant life. He is still the Master Gardener of dreams.

Paul tells us, "For we are God's masterpiece. He created us anew in Christ Jesus, so we can do the good things he planned for us long ago" (Ephesians 2:10, NLT).

Friend, you are His masterpiece. You are His beloved creation, beautifully crafted for purpose. You are a living work of art, displaying His creativity and grace.

You are not forgotten. Your dreams are not accidents. They are divine seeds, planted with intention by the Master Creator, the Master Gardener Himself.

Maybe your dream has been buried for years—under the weight of busyness, fear, disappointment, or the harsh words of others. Maybe you have convinced yourself it's too late, or you are not good enough, or your time has passed.

God says differently.

Your dream is not dead—it's dormant.

It's standing by for the season to bloom, waiting for His breath to bring it to life again.

Whether your passion is writing, singing, painting, teaching, parenting, leading, or quietly encouraging others, God delights in bringing joy to your soul. The dreams He plants are never wasted; they simply rest until His timing is right.

Our timing demands progress. His timing develops depth.

Our timing hurries. His timing ripens.

Our timing anxiously asks, "Why isn't this happening yet?"

His timing confidently whispers, "Wait—something unseen is growing."

When it's our timing, fruit feels forced. When it's His timing, fruit is inevitable. And here's the hope: even when we try to rush or force a dream, God still uses it. Nothing is wasted. He redeems every step, turning our efforts into strength and lasting joy.

Pause for a moment: where in your dream might God be using your impatience or your hurried attempts to grow something beautiful?

Take a deep breath. Step into the garden of faith. Pick up the pen. Join the choir. Start the class. Step onto the stage. Click *Register.*

No step is too small when taken in obedience—God waters it, and growth follows in His timing.

The Master Gardener is calling you by name. He holds your future, and even before you were born, He planned your destiny.

You are His masterpiece—and He is already in your tomorrow.

Sit with that truth for a moment.

Can you remember your dreams? Did you bury them beneath disappointment or fear? The ones you've buried deep under the soil of "not enough"? Can you still feel their faint heartbeat? Do they seem just out of reach?

Maybe you've poured too much dirt over your seed of hope.

God hasn't forgotten. He's still tending to the soil. He's still working beneath the surface.

He loves you and sees you, my friend. And it brings Him joy to awaken the dreams He planted in your soul.

He still truly delights in you, and He still loves bringing life to what was once lost.

Because that's who He is—the Redeemer of lost dreams. The Healer of hearts. The Restorer of joy.

You don't have to be brave enough on your own—you only need to trust the One who is.

You can step into your dream because of who Jesus is—and what He's already done.

So step forward.

Trust the Gardener.

And watch as He breathes life into the seeds you thought were gone.

He calls you beloved.

He sees the dreams still breathing beneath the soil.

And now, dear one—

It's time to bloom.

You've just walked with me through the garden of memory—from buried dreams to resurrected faith, from fear to surrender. Just as I have seen God work in my own soil, He is at work in yours.

Take a moment and look at your own story—notice where He is quietly moving beneath the surface.

Where do you see the Master Gardener at work?

Maybe you're standing in the middle of a dry season, wondering if anything good could ever grow again. Maybe you've buried a dream so deep that you've forgotten what it even looks like. Or maybe, like me, you've felt the gentle nudge of God whispering, *It's time to trust Me again.*

The truth is, God never wastes a seed. Not one tear, not one prayer, not one season of silence.

As you rest in His presence, consider these heart-questions:

1. What dream or passion did God place in your heart long ago that now feels buried or forgotten?

2. What fears, disappointments, or lies have caused you to believe that dream is "too late" or "not for you?"

3. Can you identify a season in your life when God was working beneath the surface, even though you couldn't see growth at the time?

4. Who have been the "gardeners" God used to water your dream—teachers, mentors, friends, or encouragers?

5. What small act of obedience might God be inviting you to take right now (your own version of "clicking register")?

6. How does viewing God as the Master Gardener change the way you see your waiting, fear, or silence?

7. Spend a moment in prayer, offering your buried dreams back to God. Ask Him to show you the next faithful step.

Let His Spirit bring to mind those long-forgotten places. Picture Him kneeling beside the garden of your soul, His hands in the soil, His eyes filled with love. He's not impatient with your pace. He's not frustrated by your fear. He knows exactly what you need to grow. Take one small step today, trusting Him to water it.

A Prayer for Hope and Revival

Heavenly Father,

Thank You for being the Master Gardener of my life—the One who plants dreams, knows the desires of my heart, prunes gently, and brings beauty from the soil of my story.

Forgive me for the times I've let fear, disappointment, and comparison choke out Your seeds of purpose. Thank You for never abandoning the garden of my soul, even when I neglected it.

Lord, I invite You to breathe life into every dormant dream. Awaken and revive what has been buried beneath regret or fear. Let Your living water flow to the seeds You have planted, through the cracks of my heart, and restore joy to my spirit.

You are the Master Gardener, and I trust You to tend the soil of my soul.

Bring living water to the seeds You've planted.

Teach me to trust Your timing—to believe that even in waiting, You are working. Remind me that Your plans for me are good, and Your love is constant.

Jesus, You are my peace, my Redeemer, my Joy.

Help me to rest in Your care and to walk boldly in courage and faith into the dreams You hold for me, knowing You've already gone before me, and You hold my future.

May I bloom where You've planted me—for Your glory and Your story.

In Jesus' name, Amen.

Chapter 4

Where Hope Belongs

by Kristi May

Ten years ago, I walked through one of the darkest valleys of my life. It felt like I was losing everything all at once, and no matter what I did, nothing got better. Hope was a foreign concept, and for a long time, I couldn't let my heart reach for it.

Then, a divine moment changed everything—a moment that propelled me forward and continues to guide me as I take steps toward the bright future God has for me.

It feels like a lifetime ago. Back then, after four years of chronic and clinical insomnia, I was desperate for help and also facing a heartbreaking separation from my ex-husband.

The stress of separation and of not being able to resolve our marital issues on top of years of not sleeping correctly caused my body to experience what doctors described as psychosis.

Psychosis is more prevalent among drug and alcohol users and more rarely occurs during stressful circumstances, trauma, or even pregnancy. Since the diagnosis is more frequently assigned to people who are drug and alcohol abusers, there is a high degree of shame and confusion that comes with it. For me, it took a while to even get a diagnosis, and I'm not proud to admit that I stayed in a psychiatric hospital on a 301 hold twice—a rare temporary mental health hold used when individuals are unable to care for themselves due to mental illness. Personally, I did not resist help but was required to stay at the hospital for a few days each time.

Coming home after the second hospital stay, I was 90 pounds at 5'8" and severely depressed. I never looked or felt worse. Some women in the church misunderstood my struggle and speculated about my mental health. Their words cut deeply.

Those were the hardest days of my life. The loneliness, the judgment, and the fear felt unbearable.

I always considered myself a pretty resilient person, but once I was labeled by doctors and wasn't given any hope of improvement, it was terrifying to wonder if my mind and emotions would ever return to normal. My mind wasn't as sharp as it once was. I was bombarded with thoughts about whether or not I deserved what was happening to me and whether or not God was rejecting me like my ex-husband was.

Truth be told, at one point, it felt like I was teetering on the edge of something I couldn't come back from. That's when I called out to God for help and begged Him for complete and pervasive healing. I had seen enough doctors and been prescribed enough ineffective medication to know that my true healing would only come from God.

A Divine Confirmation

During this time, I was immersing myself in scripture about healing. I remember a few verses in particular that stood out to me. I can't really say why I was drawn to these verses, but it seemed like somehow they kept being highlighted. These verses felt a bit mysterious but also pointed to Jesus as my healer.

Isaiah 53:5, ESV

*"But he was pierced for our transgressions; he was crushed for our iniquities; upon him was the chastisement that brought us peace, and **with his wounds we are healed."*** (emphasis added)

The verse above is an Old Testament prophecy, but the one below it, from the New Testament, shows the Old Testament prophecy fulfilled in Jesus.

1 Peter 2:24, ESV

*"He himself bore our sins in his body on the tree, that we might die to sin and live to righteousness. **By his wounds you have been healed."*** (emphasis added)

Since a lot of what I was battling spiritually, emotionally, and mentally was in my mind, I prayed God would renew my mind through His truth and Scripture. I wanted discernment and to know God and His will for my life. For that reason, the verse below was also one that I meditated on.

Romans 12:2, ESV

"Do not be conformed to this world, but be transformed by the renewal of your mind, that by testing you may discern what is the will of God, what is good and acceptable and perfect."

Suddenly, I began to see those verses everywhere I looked—and in the most random of places. I heard the verses in church, on Bible apps, or a stranger would reference them—and I was probably seeing them on things like Christian t-shirts, coffee mugs, and encouragement cards.

I also remember sensing in my spirit that God wanted to heal me—and very quickly, I started to experience emotional and physical healing in a variety of ways.

Emotional healing is not something that you can necessarily readily demonstrate, though physically, I did start to sleep consistently through the night for the first time in years.

While I was physically and emotionally healing, my ex-husband was setting conditions and expectations for our relationship that I couldn't meet. It was painful to feel him slipping away from me after twelve years of marriage, as he scoffed at the ways God was changing me. It was painful because I was telling the truth, but he didn't have faith. I couldn't prove what God was doing in me—there was no evidence I could show—only the quiet assurance that He was the one doing the work to change and heal me.

God was working in my life, but the timing of my healing wasn't what my ex-husband wanted.

While I was absolutely full of grief over the loss of my marriage and even a job loss, I was still putting my trust in the Lord for more miracles. It's almost as if the losses I was experiencing were causing me to have more faith because I knew I was completely powerless to help myself.

On one October day in Philadelphia's Washington Square Park, I sat on a bench with my friend, telling her about the things God was doing in my life. I remember sitting in the sunshine, eating lunch slowly, trying to put into words what I felt God was doing in my heart. I was fragile—heartbroken, yet somehow a little hopeful.

I told her that I couldn't prove it, but I thought God was healing me. Then I told her how I'd repeatedly seen the same Bible verses, as almost a confirmation, and I specifically told her that I had seen "By his wounds you have been healed" *everywhere.*

Just then, she shifted her gaze and let out a shriek as she did so. I turned to look in her direction: behind our park bench was a book in the grass, with the cover facing up. The title read, **"By his wounds you have been healed."**

Inside the book was story after story of miraculous healing as people called on the name of Jesus.

Chills ran down my body instantly.

I remember feeling confused at first, wondering if what I saw was real. The notion that divine moments like this were only for other people was definitely being challenged. I didn't feel healed in that moment, but I knew that God saw me, heard me, and loved me right where I was.

From Suffering to Restoration

That day, God gave me something concrete to hold on to when I felt so unloved and unsupported. God did prove to me that He was doing the work in me, but He also graciously let a dear friend witness what I was saying, to let me and others know *I wasn't crazy.*

I do believe God reveals Himself first and foremost through Scripture. Therefore, if you're seeking Him, reading His Word is always a great place to start. However, as someone who knows scripture, I've often been asked why I think God showed up in that way for me—but I don't have just one answer.

First, I think that God loves to reveal Himself to those who repent and those who earnestly seek Him, which I was doing. I think He is full of compassion for those who are depressed and desperate for Him, and I know that at that time in my life, I was never lower. In God's goodness, He allowed me to be encouraged and sense His presence through encountering His power.

This thought is beautifully echoed in something Charity Cook, a speaker with Global Awakening, shared with me in a private message. She said, "God's power is often displayed in the midst of suffering—and separately, suffering leads to greater intimacy with God when we turn to God in the midst of it."

God also cares about our transformation, and since that day, my life has certainly changed. I've never stopped having boldness in sharing my testimony and telling others about Jesus and what I personally have experienced.

No, God didn't reconcile my ex-husband and me—and that reality will always be difficult for me. However, God has been there for me through both the valleys and the mountain top experiences. My pain has not been wasted.

He's walked me through insomnia and psychosis, through divorce, job losses, the death of my dad after his eighteen-year struggle with Parkinson's disease, and other difficult life circumstances—most of which occurred around the same time.

He has redeemed my life in ways I could never have imagined. He has restored my confidence, my health, my courage, and has recently blessed me with a marriage to a good and Godly man.

In so many ways, it has felt like God is restoring "...the years that the swarming locust has eaten..." (Joel 2:25, ESV).

The Tension Between Suffering and Healing

I share this part of my story thoughtfully, because I know not everyone experiences healing in the ways I have. Some may still be waiting, wondering why God feels silent or why their circumstances haven't changed. I've struggled with this tension myself —wanting to hope for good things while also knowing that, as believers, we are sometimes called to suffer.

The biggest outcome of my trials was that I learned to put my trust in God, not man. Still, I wrestle with fully understanding why I experienced what I did physically and spiritually—and why God graciously chose to heal and restore me. It took me years to come to a place where I can say this honestly, but I have learned that God is good, even when life includes hard and unwanted circumstances. The character of God is good, even when things don't make sense.

There is no doubt that we are sometimes called to suffer, as Jesus did—and even to be misunderstood or perceived as "crazy." Scripture is filled with individuals who were asked to do things that appeared outrageous to others, often at great personal cost. Noah building the ark and Joshua marching around Jericho come to mind as examples of radical obedience despite public perception—there are hundreds of other examples. Their stories remind us that God's promises do not depend on how things appear or how we feel, but on the unchanging character of God.

There have been seasons when God has blessed me with the outcome I prayed for, and others when His answer looked very different from what I wanted. Sometimes the unexpected blessings were far better than what I had imagined for my life. Other times, learning new things about God brought a joy that outweighed the circumstances I did not desire. Jesus promised trouble in this world, and following Him does not guarantee prosperity or healing.

Yet there is no greater thing than the love of God for us. My hope is that my desire to know God and be known by Him will always outweigh my desire for any favorable outcome.

Through my own journey, I've discovered three truths that can serve as a roadmap for anyone facing trials—truths that can bring hope, clarity, and action.

1. **Healing requires putting your hope in God.** At some point in my healing, I had to confront where I was placing my hope. I had leaned on

people, on systems, on my own ability to fix what was broken—and each of those supports eventually fell short. True healing began when I learned to place my hope fully in God, not in man. That did not mean rejecting help or denying medication, counseling, or wise guidance. It meant recognizing that none of those things is necessarily the source of transformation. In a culture saturated with self-help formulas and manifestation language that tells us to look inward for power, Scripture calls us to look upward. Change did not come because I finally figured it out; it came because I surrendered control and trusted that the Lord could change what I could not.

So I want to gently ask you: are you sick, anxious, or depressed? Is your marriage in need of restoration? Are you powerless to break a habit or a hidden area of sin? Put your hope in God. Not in people. Not in doctors alone. Not in your own strength. Bring your need to the One who is able to heal, restore, and strengthen you. Seek Him honestly, invite Him into the places you have tried to manage on your own, and allow Him to do the work only He can do. You may not control the process, but you will never regret placing your hope in the God who meets you with grace and sustains you with His strength.

2. **Beyond hope, healing requires action.** In John 5, Jesus encounters a man who had been disabled for thirty-eight years and asks him a question that feels almost uncomfortable in

its simplicity: "Do you want to get well?" (John 5:6, CSB). The man responds by explaining his circumstances—how no one helps him, how others always get there first, how the system meant to heal him has failed. His reasons are understandable. They are human. Yet Jesus does not engage the excuses or debate the fairness of the situation. Instead, He speaks an invitation that carries both compassion and responsibility: "Get up... pick up your mat and walk" (John 5:8, CSB). Healing, in that moment, required more than hope—it required participation.

I have witnessed this same crossroads in people who have endured psychosis, severe insomnia, divorce, and deep emotional or spiritual trauma - journeys I know personally. There is profound grace for the pain people carry, and there is also a quiet truth that cannot be ignored: no one can do the work for you. While God healed me in undeniable ways, my restoration also involved obedience through process—seeking medical care, committing to counseling for years, and showing up daily to do the hard work of healing. Like the man at the pool, healing often begins when we stop waiting for conditions to change and start responding to the invitation to take action. Sometimes that means repentance. Sometimes it means examining patterns we've repeated for years or courageously tracing wounds back to their roots. Whether the work is emotional, spiritual, or physical, healing asks us not to run from the hard parts but to engage them. Wanting to get well is not about self-reliance—it is about obedience and the willingness to move forward. If you find yourself at the crossroads, please don't quit—do your part.

3. **You are never too damaged to be used by God.** For a long time, I believed that what I had been through had permanently disqualified me. In the middle of healing—when my mind, heart, and identity were still being reshaped—I felt damaged, exposed, and unsure of how God could ever use a story like mine. My journey included mental health struggles, a frightening diagnosis, and a marriage that ended when my husband left. Those are the kinds of details people can misunderstand or reduce to labels. It would have been easier to stay quiet, to protect myself from being seen as "too much" or "too broken." Yet even in that uncertainty, I sensed that God was not finished with me. I did not know when— or how—He would allow me to share my story, but I trusted that He would redeem it in His time.

What I have learned is this: no story is too messy for God to shine through. Healing does not erase the past; it transforms it into testimony. God does not wait for us to feel polished or put back together before He uses us—He works through the very places we once thought disqualified us. If you feel damaged, sidelined, or afraid that your story is too complicated to be redeemed, know this: you are not beyond God's reach or purpose. Even the most fragile stories can bring hope when they are surrendered to God.

No Coincidences

In sharing this story of mine, my desire is that you would be reminded that God is powerful and so very personal and active in our lives. He is still doing miracles, He is still healing people, and He isn't excluding you. His plan for our lives is for our good.

Just like my own experience back in the park, I don't think you are holding this book by accident. If you, too, are facing something hard and are in need of a miracle, of God's goodness, and of grace, I hope this testimony and encouragement have reached you at just the right moment—because I know God's timing is that perfect.

Next Steps

Take a moment to pause and reflect honestly on where you are right now. Healing often begins with awareness and willingness.

First, ask yourself: Have I truly decided that I want to get well, or have I been waiting for someone else—or something else—to change first? What step is God asking me to take, even if it feels uncomfortable or small?

Next, consider where your hope is anchored. Are you placing it in people, outcomes, or your own ability to fix what feels broken? Or are you bringing your need to God and trusting Him to work in ways you cannot control? Invite Him into the places where you feel most powerless and ask for His help.

Finally, reflect on how you see your own story. Have you surrendered it to God, or are you still hiding parts of it out of fear or shame? You are not too damaged to be used by

Him. Ask God to show you where He may want to use your experiences—whether quietly or publicly, now or later. Ask Him to give you the courage to trust His timing. Simply offer yourself as you are, and allow God to do the rest.

Chapter 5

Ashes to Beauty, Beauty to Ashes

by Elizabeth Bass

Many years ago, life became almost too hard to survive. It still brings tears to my eyes when I remember. Perhaps it's especially poignant because, as I write this, we're approaching the time of year when it hurts the most—Christmas time.

Mamma was a beautiful lady. Oh, she would vehemently disagree. When she looked in the mirror, she would frequently announce that she was fat and ugly. It always troubled me when she said that. She was a gentle, compassionate soul who reached out to friends and strangers alike and ministered to everyone she met. That made her beautiful in my eyes.

It seemed impossible that anything could turn my mamma's beauty into ashes. But cancer did the impossible.

Her body began a slow, cruel process of eating her up from the inside out.

When it became clear that death would likely be the inevitable outcome, but the cancer had not yet consumed her ability to think clearly, Mamma focused on what we would need after she was gone. It was her desire to donate her remains to the University of Pennsylvania to learn how to fight this cancer better in other patients in the future. My brother Tim and I expressed a need to have a final resting place where we could go to grieve the loss of our mother. So arrangements were made and legal documents signed for her ashes to be returned to us when the university was finished with her remains. Plans were made to take her ashes to the homestead in West Virginia and scatter them there. Grandma prepared a special place for this purpose.

There came a point when Mamma needed to be hospitalized. Unfortunately, the people who should have cared and helped were unwilling to do what they were able in order to curb the cancer's appetite. They neglected to care for her properly when we entrusted her to their care.

This became very evident to me one night when I went to the hospital to see her. She didn't want medication that would diminish her mental awareness, but the hospital insisted on keeping her sedated so that fewer nurses would be needed on the unit. I walked into her room and found her sound asleep. The IV fluid bag was empty, and her blood had gone up the tube. It had been that way so long that the blood had dried inside the tube. I was very angry, but I knew that my parents would not want me to say anything about it. I pushed the call button for the nurse and told her that the IV bag was empty. She came into the room, woke Mamma up out of a sound sleep, and asked in an accusatory voice, "Mrs. Richards, why didn't you tell me this was like this?" My mother's groggy reply was an apology.

I was furious! I wanted to hold the hospital staff accountable and make them own up to their blatant neglect to help Mamma fight against this fire that raged within her and ravaged her body mercilessly! But Mom and Dad would never permit it. They always assumed people were doing their best and needed to be pardoned for their shortcomings, even when, to me, negligence was blatant and inexcusable. So the fire consumed her more cruelly and more rapidly than should have been permitted, leaving embers of horrible grief and compounded resentment to burn within my own soul.

When we brought her home to take care of her ourselves, the hospital staff failed to supply us with the level of knowledge and medications necessary to ease her pain properly and help her fight the cancer. Although we did our best with the skills and equipment we were given, it seemed to me we failed her miserably, with the cancer taking full advantage of our ignorance and limitations.

Over the Christmas holidays, many of our relatives came to say their goodbyes. I was stunned by the reactions of my family members. Several of them stayed in Mamma's room for only seconds before they came flying out of the room. Some of them ran straight to the bathroom because the odor was so pungent. I had never noticed the odor until then. Others would cry uncontrollably because of how horrible she looked. It was shocking to see these reactions and hear what they said. She was my mamma! To me, she was still precious, and there could never be anything repulsive about her!

Mamma died on January 2, 1980. For three days before she passed away, she saw Heaven's door and pleaded continually for someone to open the door and let her in. She would cry out desperately, "Open it further! I can't get in! Please! Open a window!"

It broke my heart to hear it, and it seemed to me that God was very cruel to leave her lingering like that. If He wasn't going to heal her, at least He should have the kindness to answer her pleas. But when the end finally came, she was at peace. She took one final breath, and she was gone.

At the time of her death, I wasn't home. My family had insisted that I go with my uncle to the airport in Philadelphia, Pennsylvania, to pick up my oldest brother, his wife, and one week old baby, and my fiancé. My brother and his family were supposed to arrive from Omaha, Nebraska, but their flight had been canceled, and they had been rerouted several times so that they ended up flying in from Florida. Their luggage had been lost along the way, so we had to file papers to have it sent to our house. My brother's wife needed some things that were in the luggage, so we had to stop at a store. One after another, the delays piled up. I was anxious to get back to Mamma. Eventually, I would see that these interruptions were important to God's plan. At the moment, they were facing obstacles to getting back home.

It was nighttime when we finally arrived home. I was about to collapse from exhaustion. As we pulled into the driveway, we saw a black station wagon parked there. I said,

"I wonder who we know who drives a black station wagon?" Then I realized that Mamma was gone. I was instantly consumed with grief and guilt. I hadn't even been home when she died! I couldn't bear to go inside. My father came out and tried to convince me to come in, but I refused. He asked me, "Don't you want to come in and see her before they take her away?" I said something like, "I've watched her dying for four months. I don't need to see her now."

From a distance, I watched as the men put Mamma's body in their car and drove away. I would never see her again until Heaven.

Over the next week, while my brother and his family were there, the presence of the newborn baby eased the absence of Mamma. One of her greatest desires was to be a grandma, and this delicate darling was her first grandchild. She had been trapped inside her struggling body for all of those months. Now her spirit was free to celebrate her new status as "grandmother." It was a great mercy from her Heavenly Father.

Many months later, I realized that God's timing was perfect. If Mamma had died any sooner, my brother would never have been able to say goodbye to her before the men took her away. I think it was important for him to see the extent of the harm the cancer had done to her for his own grieving process. But if she had not died before we got home from the airport, he would have seen her suffering, crying out for Heaven, struggling for every breath, along with all of the trauma that our other family members experienced at the sight of her. I don't know how he could have stood it. God, in His mercy, had spared my brother that level of trauma. Even though it seemed to me that God was cruel to Mamma, in truth, He was being merciful to my brother. Mamma would have wanted it that way.

Immediately after her death, I experienced a severe physical collapse. Even the nutrients stored in my bones had been completely depleted. I slept twenty hours or more every day for several days. I ran a fever for months, and I caught every illness with which I came in contact.

The time came for the spring semester to begin, and that presented a dilemma. My doctor insisted that I shouldn't try to attend classes that spring. However, my mamma was very emphatic that I should complete my education no matter what. She had dropped out in her senior year of college when she married Dad. They both had determined for her to resume classes to finish her degree as soon as possible. "As soon as possible" didn't come until all four of us children were in high school. Because of how long she had been delayed, she was enrolled as a sophomore and had to repeat many classes. How could I ignore what was so important to her, especially so near to her death?

I was eighteen credits shy of graduation. I felt I absolutely had to do it! I gave it my best effort, but I missed many classes and got lower grades on the projects I did. I actually failed one class and had to make it up that summer. Mom had always been my cheerleader and always encouraged me to do my best. The absence of that intensified my sense of loss.

I held onto the thought that once I finished my education, life would get easier and I would be able to rest.

Unfortunately, that was not the case. Life brought new challenges and more intense grief and trauma.

I got married five months after Mamma died. I believed my marriage would be a safe haven where I could take time to recover, but it didn't turn out that way. Instead, my marriage compounded my troubles. Just one week after the wedding, I discovered that the man who had been a source of security and stability during Mamma's sickness and death had a hidden, violent temper. I got pregnant in less than a month after the wedding and lost that baby because my body wasn't capable of nurturing a fetus at that time.

My husband decided to start seminary that fall, so we moved to Philadelphia. I took a teaching position in New Jersey about sixty miles away. Less than a month later, I became pregnant again. I was very sick and lost thirty pounds during the ten months of pregnancy. When the baby was born, she had lost at least a pound from the deterioration of the placenta. During the birthing process, she got pneumonia from an infection in the amniotic fluid. She was born in a small town in New Jersey. She was transferred to a NICU in Philadelphia when she was about twenty hours old. My OB/GYN wanted me to stay in the hospital for a longer period of time, but once my baby was taken to the other hospital, there was nothing that could keep me from going to be with her.

It was kind of comical when the morning after she was transferred, the nurses found me up, dressed, packed, and ready to go at 6:30 a.m. My room was right next to the nurses' station, so I heard my doctor's voice when he arrived around eight o'clock. The nurses told him how anxious I was to leave. He managed to find other things to attend to until almost noon. He finally came into my room and tried to convince me to stay longer, but I was adamant. My father came to take me to his house soon after the doctor left, and he also tried to get me to stay longer. There was no way I would comply. Even after leaving the hospital, Dad insisted I eat lunch and rest. Finally, at around 7 p.m. that evening, he consented to take me to see my baby.

She was so tiny and frail; all hooked up to tubes and machines and lying in an incubator. The nurses situated all of the things to which she was hooked up and let me hold her while I sat in a rocking chair. Eventually, I had to give her back and go back to Dad's house. I was extremely depleted and barely able to climb the small steps to the door at around 12:30 a.m. I collapsed onto my old bed and slept through the next day and night. Nobody was willing to wake me up. Once my daughter was stabilized, she healed quickly, and in two weeks, I was able to take her home.

The time came when the University of Pennsylvania said that it would have completed its research. Dad was to receive a phone call informing him that he could come and get Mamma's ashes. That time came and went without a word. Dad was patient, trusting that the word would come soon. What finally came was an impostor in the form of a letter telling us that Mamma's ashes had been mixed with the ashes of thirty other people and placed at marker #76 in Mount Peace Cemetery in the middle of Philadelphia. When Dad called to ask why this was done without first calling him, as agreed upon prior to Mom's death, he was told that he should have called to remind them of this agreement. This left Dad feeling that he had let Mamma down; instead of the University taking responsibility for their own breach of contract. The fire that had turned my mamma's beauty into ashes burned on within my own heart and soul, ravaging me with unbearable grief and anger.

Still, the list of traumas and illnesses piled one on top of another until I felt like I was getting buried in them. I struggled to function in a very dysfunctional marriage. I had five children in eight years, nursing each one into the next pregnancy. That overtaxed my already weakened body even more, resulting in repeated hospitalizations. I struggled to be a faithful servant to my Lord and Savior while I tried to be the best wife and mother I could be.

After the birth of my second son, my fifth surviving baby, I suffered from postpartum depression, which was the beginning of decades in mental health care. There were moments of crisis when I thought I would lose my family. Eventually, I divorced my husband. Through all those years, there was no opportunity to move through the grief of my mother's death. When I look back, I can't fathom how I coped with it all. I know now, as I knew then, that God was with me, holding me up and carrying me through.

For a long time, I had no interest in visiting the cemetery where my mamma's ashes were buried. I was angry and resentful that they were mixed with other people—strangers only linked to us through the sacrifice they made along with Mamma for the purpose of scientific advancement. The fact that the University didn't live up to their agreement with Mom and Dad remained a thorn in my side for a very long time, hindering my own healing process. It would be many years before I could bring myself to go visit the place where my mamma's ashes had been placed. It was in a huge city instead of the place we had all anticipated. Mamma would never have wanted to be in a city. She was a West Virginia hillbilly, and we all loved that part of our heritage.

When the time came for me to visit my mamma's grave site, I called the cemetery to let them know I would be coming. When we got there, we found a freshly mowed area in a far corner. There was a small piece of cement about 3" x 5" and about a quarter inch thick with the number "76" pressed into it. The cement had been broken, perhaps by the weight of a lawnmower. My heart ached afresh at the obvious lack of care and appreciation for the sacrifice of the thirty-one people who had given their bodies to be studied at the University, and the lack of respect for their families. As I tenderly placed a bouquet that I had created and a copy of the tribute I had written near the marker, I listened to the birds happily conversing in the trees all around me and the sound of children playing at a nearby daycare. Now that was something Mamma would have definitely enjoyed. She had been a teacher of preschool special-needs children, and she had enjoyed that immensely. She had enriched the lives of many young children and their families. This was something positive that I could be thankful for in the presence of Mamma's final resting place. It was a soothing balm on a still-hurting wound. I could walk away thankful.

I live many miles away from Philadelphia. I can't go visit the cemetery when I want to be near where my mamma's remains are buried. I don't feel the need to return. It's not what we wanted; it's not what it should have been, but it is what it is. I'm not angry anymore. I'm at peace with my mamma's remains being located in Mount Peace Cemetery in the heart of Philadelphia.

The ashes are not the end of the story for Mamma or for me. Death for her brought sweet relief and comfort in the arms of her Jehovah Rapha—the God Who heals. Never again would she see herself as fat or ugly, because from that moment on, she would only see her reflection in the adoring eyes of her Savior, Jesus Christ.

For me, Mamma's death set the stage for many years of trauma—years when other fires fanned the flames of Mamma's death, never letting them fade to embers and cool. Like a forest that has been ravaged by an all-consuming fire, little by little, new beginnings of growth have emerged. Once mighty oaks of right and wrong are being replaced with tender young shoots that bend instead of breaking when the storms of life blow hard against them.

I have learned to accept these words in Ecclesiastes 3:1–2, 4, and 11 (ESV): "For everything there is a season, and a time for every matter under heaven: a time to be born, and a time to die;... a time to weep, and a time to laugh; a time to mourn, and a time to dance;...He has made everything beautiful in its time."

Next Steps:

Write a goodbye letter to your deceased parent. Be extremely honest about your feelings. Release them to your heavenly Father's hands. Then say a prayer for God to guide you through your healing process.

Chapter 6

Unwinding the Graveclothes: A Story of Deliverance and Newfound Identity

by Elaine Lopez

"BUT NOW THUS SAYS THE LORD, HE WHO CREATED YOU,
O JACOB, HE WHO FORMED YOU, O ISRAEL:
'FEAR NOT, FOR I HAVE REDEEMED YOU;
I HAVE CALLED YOU BY NAME, YOU ARE MINE.'"
ISAIAH 43:1 (ESV)

The hardest part wasn't the violation; it was him calling my name, inviting me into his room, asking me to strum my fingers across his guitar as he closed the door behind me, using my own innocence against me. He knew I loved that guitar. That was the weapon of choice. That large, smooth, familiar electric Fender was now transformed into a trap. The texture of the sharp, cold guitar strings bit into my fingers as if alerting me to the danger I was in. The smell of dust and old wood mingled with cologne and the sweetness of chewing gum as he whispered my name—it was all embedded in my memory as a final remnant of childhood innocence.

Looking back, I can still hear the sharp click of the door snapping tightly behind me. The silence engulfed every sound in the room except the laughter of my sisters playing next door. The sharp click became a sound that for many years meant safety was being locked out—and something much colder was being locked in.

At eight years of age, I lived a simple life: going to school, playing tag with friends, riding bikes, reading books, and spending time with family. I was carefree, imaginative, and lived fully present in the moment. My only worries were whether to play a game of tag or decide which book to read next. I could walk to school without fear, trusting that the adults around me would keep me safe from harm. Fear was a foreign concept, far removed from my reality. It held no space in my world of make-believe, brimming full with adventures and endless possibilities. I only understood hope and joy, fully convinced that life was perfect, trusting the adults when they said I would always be safe.

At such a young age, I didn't understand the concept of faith. It was a fragile, loose thread that could unravel at any moment; one tug, and it would all fall apart. In my family, church attendance was non-negotiable, a rigid daily routine that left no room to breathe. I was the straggler, always waiting until the last second to get ready. My parents would find me buried under the covers, my nose in a book, lost in a world that didn't demand my silence. The Church was supposed to be a place to meet God, but certain stipulations were the foundation of good church etiquette—

designed, they claimed, to ensure strong, moral character. No pants allowed. Long hair only. No makeup or jewelry can be worn. No movies, dancing, or television. Submit to authority. Always carry the appearance of holiness. Except appearances can be deceiving.

Appearances can masquerade as moral superiority. The Bible speaks about people who appear outwardly religious while inwardly hiding a corrupt, deceitful heart. In the book of Matthew, Jesus confronts the Pharisees and condemns them for carrying a false mask of righteousness. The Pharisees were teachers and leaders of local synagogues who would seek the Law for loopholes to protect themselves while exerting more control over the people. Anyone who dared to defy their rulings was severely punished. Jesus despised their deceitful actions and called the Pharisees "hypocrites" because on the outside they pretended to be holy and righteous, but on the inside their hearts were evil, unclean, and corrupt. Pharisees were hiding among members of my church. My sexual abuser was one of them.

He was ten years older than me, and our families spent time together sharing meals and hobbies, becoming very close over the years. The family was actively involved in church activities and knew everyone in the congregation. They were kind, funny, and loving, making you feel welcomed in their presence. But the father held to rigid standards of modesty and holiness. The women laughed, but behind their smiles, I could sense fear. In this family, there were several older daughters who would let my sisters and me play dress-up in their room and apply makeup. I found it exciting and fun to pretend to be all grown-up.

They also had an older son. His room was directly across from them. He was always quiet, always watching. It made me uncomfortable. But I was also curious about what cool things he possibly had in his room. It was always locked. Until one day, the door was left slightly ajar. I could see the outline of two things: a bed and an electric Fender guitar leaning against it. The guitar instantly drew my attention. Suddenly, he appeared.

He eased the door open, his eyes locked on mine with a strong intensity. "Want to see it?" He gestured toward the silver electric guitar, lightly touching my hand, a strange reverence in his touch. His voice was barely above a whisper, inviting me into his private world, a world I suddenly didn't want to see. I felt a pit of unease form in my belly, a warning bell on full alert, as I looked at his unreadable expression and quickly looked away. Averting my eyes, I forced my chin down in a single, stiff nod: "Yes." He wrapped his large hand around mine, snapping the door shut behind us.

I instantly smelled sweet mint mingled with cologne as he bent down in front of me, his breath fanning my hair. "Would you like to play the guitar?" I knew this didn't feel right. I felt nauseating, fluttering panic in my chest, making it difficult to focus and breathe. Despite the panic, my desire to play the guitar was stronger. I quickly looked at the guitar and said, "I would, yes." He led me closer to his bed, his hand pressed hard against my back, quickly walking me to its edge.

Lifting the guitar off the floor, he positioned it directly across the bed. "Before you can play, I need you to lie down on my bed first." I could hear buzzing in my head, a loud ringing in my ears, as he pulled me closer. He pushed the guitar over and motioned me to rest beside it. With shallow breaths and shaky knees, I climb up onto the bed and lie very still, like a mannequin afraid to move a muscle. My small body was engulfed in the huge bed. I felt lost, scared, and alone. Closing my eyes tightly, I pretended I was in one of my books, far away in another world.

Seconds pass by very slowly as I feel the mattress dip beneath the weight of his body, climbing in beside me. Intense shaking overwhelms my entire body as his fingers touch my belly, my chest, my cheek, following back down across my legs. I can't speak, or scream, or utter a word. The fear has silenced my vocal cords. He shifts his weight to lie on top of me. He presses himself fully against me, and I lie limp, my mind lost in another world where I can't be hurt. His lips, sweetened with a taste of mint I will always hate, crush against my own, his tongue seeking a way in. The pain of his body and his lips forcibly stealing my innocence was beyond what I could bear. It was like a switch came on, and I was back in my body, alert and angry. I opened my mouth, and with every bit of strength in my tiny body, I slammed down my teeth and bit his tongue. He quickly yelped in pain, rearing his head back, gripping his tongue, which was bleeding. I scrambled out from beneath him and ran out of the room. I nearly tripped over my feet as I flung myself down the steps and burst into the living room, where both my family and his were enjoying some coffee and laughing together. I screamed, "He touched me!" over and over, unable to speak any other words. He was not too far behind me. Silence filled the room; only gasps of my breath could be heard. Suddenly, my mom screamed, and all chaos broke loose. The sound of high-pitched screams, hysterical cries, desperate pleas of confusion, and looks of shock and pain permeated every available space in the room that day. What happened in that room irrevocably changed me forever.

When trauma occurs, it is normal to feel pain, anger, and confusion. God is not indifferent to your emotions. He is present with you in the suffering and pain, not distant or gone. The trauma and shame experienced due to sexual assault and abuse do not define your identity; God does. You have inherent value and worth in God's eyes. The horrific actions committed against you are not your fault and are not factors that define who you are. You are a beloved child of God, and it is this truth that defines you. As a survivor of sexual abuse, it is important to know that God is a God of justice. The Bible clearly reveals how God hates wickedness, evil, and injustice, including abuse. Psalm 9:9–10 (NLT), which says, "The Lord is a shelter for the oppressed, a refuge in times of trouble," assures survivors that God is not blind to what was done against you and He sees the evil that occurred. He hates the sin of the abuser, and he will bring justice, for he is a refuge for you.

God is present in suffering and pain. In Psalm 34:18, we are given a picture of God's heart that is intimately present and not far from us, in our pain, showing He draws near to the "brokenhearted" and remains in the midst of the pain of all who are "crushed in spirit" (ESV). He is intentionally near and does not pull away from you when you are in deep agony and overwhelming grief from the trauma. He sees the pain and knows the weight of the grief that makes you feel like you can't breathe. The pain and suffering can cause you to feel isolated and alone, but this verse reminds you that you are not forgotten because He draws near to you and remains with you even when you are not able to express the anguish inside.

Trauma does not define your identity; God does. Isaiah 43:1 reminds you that God redeems you and calls you by your name, not by your trauma. It emphasizes His ownership of you and how every hurtful label and horrific action holds no power to claim you. This verse plants you in His redemptive love, reveals your belonging and purpose is found in Him, and that you are not defined by the trauma but by His plan for you. Trauma tries to label you as worthless and broken, but the verse declares that you belong to God, redeemed and known by the One who gave it all for you.

Trauma may have marked your life, leaving a trail of brokenness and pain, but in Christ, our deepest wounds and scars can become beacons of light where His redemptive love, grace, and healing power shine the brightest, revealing the truth of who we truly are in Him—victorious and free.

Guided Scripture and Prayer:

Scripture

Psalm 139:14 (ESV): "I praise you, for I am fearfully and wonderfully made. Wonderful are your works; my soul knows it very well."

The human body is truly amazing! It has specific ways to protect you, which are designed by God to do so. Let's consider the brain. When trauma occurs, it physically alters the brain's structure, affecting its ability to remain calm by keeping it hyperactive and in "fight or flight" mode. This leads to constant jumpiness, hypervigilance, and extreme anxiety. Living in this state of fear can make you feel disassociated from yourself, like your body is not your own. But God has made a way for the brain to heal. This way of healing is called neuroplasticity. Neuroplasticity allows the brain to strengthen connections and build healthier thought patterns when partnered with trauma-informed therapy. It is essentially "rewiring" the brain.

In the same way neuroplasticity rewires the brain, God also rewires the way you view your identity. By using faith practices such as meditating in the Word, prayer, biblical community support, and trauma-informed therapy, your brain creates new pathways to see yourself the way God says you are. Trauma-based fear responses are replaced with God's Word that reminds you that you are fearfully and wonderfully made. This transformation is a healing process that begins from the inside out, allowing you to experience both a spiritual and physical change that rewrites the trauma narrative.

God defines you, and He says you are fearfully and wonderfully made.

Prayer

Dear Heavenly Father,

You remind me that my trauma does not define me. You do. Help me trust Your Word over the lies of my abuse, and to recognize that I am designed and fearfully made by You.

When the flashbacks and the memories of the trauma return, remind me You are constant and intentionally near. Teach me to remain present in Your love and not to allow fear to speak louder than Your Word. I will do my part to stay in prayer, read Your Word, and keep connected to a biblical community. Then I will rest knowing You created me with intention and I am valuable and worthy to You.

In Jesus' name, I pray, Amen.

Chapter 7

The Redemption of a Recovering Perfectionist: A Renewal of Grace and Dependency

by Anna Grace Head

"MAY YOU OFFER GOD YOUR LACK AS THE KINDLING FOR HOLY INTIMACY, GIVING HIM THE OPPORTUNITY TO PROVE HIS GRACE, NOT LEAVING ANYTHING OUT FROM THE ALTAR OF YOUR HEART, GIVING HIM YOUR WHOLE...AND IF I FEEL NUMB, SPIRITLESS, UNSURE, AND WITHOUT FLAME, I WILL GIVE YOU ALL OF THAT TOO, UNTIL EVERY INCH OF ME IS YOURS."
—COMMONOR'S COMMUNION[1]

Wrapped in a purple blanket my grandmother had crocheted, I cuddled next to my mom on our plaid, weathered couch. I leaned my head against her arm. The familiar scent of her perfume and the latest library book enveloped me in a sense of safety and comfort. The fairy tales that we all know and love were a staple in my home. "Sleeping Beauty," "Beauty and the Beast," and "Cinderella" all made regular appearances in my childhood. What was unique, however, was the way my mom would finish reading the story. She never said, "And they all lived happily ever after" at the close of these books. Instead, my mom would say, "And they got married, had some problems, worked through them together, and grew in their love and in the strength of their marriage."

That is what I always understood to be true about fairy tales. There was no such thing as happily ever after. It was a marriage of two sinners that needed grace, forgiveness, and the intentionality to grow. So, when I got married, I knew marriage would be both difficult and beautiful. It would be sanctifying and wonderful. I did not presume to be Cinderella and ride off into the sunset to live in eternal bliss and happiness with my husband. But even with this understanding, I still stubbornly and pridefully expected myself to be the consummate wife—one who never made mistakes, disappointed, or hurt my husband. I didn't presume to be Cinderella, but I did presume to be perfect— the perfect wife, and in my case, the perfect stepmom.

Her scowling eyes, corseted, high-collared dress, and sinister expression make her one of the most recognized characters in fairytale lore. But beyond her severe appearance, her reputation precedes her—she is cruel, malicious, and, as we have all stereotyped her, wicked. Her name is Lady Tremaine. But I would venture to guess that if you knew that, you are amongst a minuscule subset of the population who do. More commonly, we simply know her as the wicked stepmother from the fairy tale "Cinderella." As I stepped into the role of stepmother, I became keenly aware of the stereotypical wicked stepmother ideology: she seems to overtake a home and family with a malignant agenda, spitefully exercises her will to control, and heartlessly steals a father's affection.

Like any stepmom who despises the wicked stereotype, I have desperately sought to control my own narrative in that role and to outrun the complexity that it presents. Having said that, my dear friend, let me introduce myself. I am a stepmom who began this journey with a history of being wildly self-reliant and the propensity to believe that I am the author of my story and the architect of my value. I am a stepmom and a wife who long ago befriended perfectionism as a reflection of my worth. I am a stepmom and a wife who has learned and is still learning that I am neither the wicked villain, hero, nor the author.

Perhaps that is where you find yourself, too—at the beginning of a story in which you are tightly gripping the pen, afraid of what it will look like to relinquish your own beliefs about your value. Perhaps you are in the middle of a story that finds you shackled to white-knuckling your way through your world, suffocating under a burden you were never meant to shoulder alone. And perhaps you, too, might need a stark but beautiful invitation to lay down the notion that you can carry and sustain everything, and to disband the idea that you can wrestle with God and win back control. If that is you, then welcome. Welcome to a once-upon-a-time that is fraught with difficulty and suffering, but that is held together by a gentle and strong Savior. Welcome to the middle of your story, where God is at work, weaving and crafting you to reflect Him more fully. Welcome to the truest happily ever after—one that ends with the redemption of all things and the spectacular reality of God making everything new.

The Seduction of Self-Sufficiency

When I was growing up, I was the "strong one," the "responsible one," and the one who never rocked the boat. I was long-suffering, and I was good at it. My family system, heartaches, and traumas taught me how to survive by running hard into and through adversity. Even everyday tasks felt like they had to be carried out flawlessly so as not to disappoint others or subvert my own sense of purpose. I took every deep and wide feeling that I had and shouldered them with quiet determination so as not to take up too much space and not need too much. Yielding my needs for the sake of anyone else's in the name of being a "good Christian" was an art that I had mastered. And anything that didn't meet my own absurdly high expectations of myself felt devastating. The cries of my heart for space were silenced, and the parts of me that longed to be seen and loved for who I was were ignored. Almost as if the very space I occupied needed justifying, I apologized for everything, even things that did not merit an apology. I believed that my worth was contingent on my ability to perform and on what I could offer—whether through my time, energy, or talents.

Yes, I grew up in a Christian home, and knew that my worth came from Jesus alone. I walked with the Lord and knew that His strength was made perfect in my weakness, but even that felt like it was my responsibility to maintain. There was an incongruence between what seemed to be the reality of life and what I was taught about the Lord. Moving into adulthood, I spent time in therapy and doing the brutal but healing work of taking up space, knowing and expressing my needs, and embracing my belovedness simply because I am a child of God. But when I became a wife and stepmom, I found myself thrown back into the battle of perfection and striving I had been fighting my entire life. Marriage and stepmotherhood shoved me in front of a mirror, and I was seeing reflected back to me all of my worst parts. To borrow another fairy tale illustration: "Mirror, mirror on the wall...who is the most prideful and self-righteously autonomous of them all?"[2]

Before we proceed, I need to rewind a bit and explain a crucial aspect of my story: I was never a girl or woman who wanted children. I never felt as though being a mother would make my life complete. I heard my friends say that they had "baby fever," but holding a baby never stirred a desire to have one of my own, and I was always rather relieved to hand a baby back to their parents. So, there I was in 2019, at the ripe old age of 32, still unmarried and childless. Yes, I wanted to be a wife, but I had found great contentment in my singleness and held marriage with open hands. Nevertheless, rattling around in the back corners of my mind was the idea that a godly woman was supposed to be a wife and mother. And if by some chance you were not, or were not by a certain age, you were somehow flawed and without purpose in the church. In July of that year, due to a complicated medical history, I had to have a total hysterectomy with a unilateral salpingo-oophorectomy. All of that medical jargon to say, I was unable to have children. I was barren. I felt a profound sense of grief and a level of internal conflict and confusion born out of that grief. I never strongly desired to have kids, so why was I feeling so heartbroken that I could not have them? I had to untangle myself from the lie that I was somehow less of a woman and less of what constituted a "godly" woman. The possibility of rejection was foreboding if any future spouse found my inability to have children to be a dealbreaker. I now held the both/and of not particularly wanting children, and the grief that I could never even consider having them. So, on a rainy afternoon, I lay curled up on the end of my bed, heart shattered in pieces, body reeling from a massive surgery, and my spirit feeling just as barren as my body. I cried out to God that I could not get to Him, and that I needed Him to come and speak tenderly to my wounded heart. I opened my Bible straight to Isaiah 54:1–6 (MSG):

"Sing, barren woman, who has never had a baby.

Fill the air with song, you who've never experienced childbirth!

You're ending up with far more children
than all those childbearing women." God says so!
"Clear lots of ground for your tents!
Make your tents large. Spread out! Think big!
Use plenty of rope,
drive the tent pegs deep.
You're going to need lots of elbow room
for your growing family.
You're going to take over whole nations;
you're going to resettle abandoned cities.
Don't be afraid—you're not going to be embarrassed.
Don't hold back—you're not going to come up short.

You'll forget all about the humiliations of your youth,
and the indignities of being a widow will fade from
memory.
For your Maker is your bridegroom,
his name, God-of-the-Angel-Armies!
Your Redeemer is The Holy of Israel,
known as God of the whole earth…"

Here I was, collapsed in the arms of my heavenly Father, and He was calling me into an embracing of my weakness—to be at peace in my literal barrenness. God was going to prove sufficient in building His kingdom through me, whether or not I could have children. Nevertheless, I prayed that if God had a spouse for me, that whoever he was would embrace me in all facets of my brokenness.

When I met my now-husband, he had primary custody of his two children from his previous marriage. He had been divorced for several years and had done the beautiful but painful work of healing from the dissolution of that marriage and his ex-wife's infidelity. He had owned his shortcomings and failings in that process, and as he walked through that, he had profoundly encountered the Lord. I could trace the redemptive work of Jesus in his life—I could see the resurrection in him. My husband did indeed embrace me in all facets of my brokenness— including my barrenness. Yes, my husband had children, but it was not a desire to fulfill some sort of maternal hole in my heart that sealed the deal, so to speak. Rather, it was my husband's heart, his desire to know and love Jesus, and out of that, to know and love me, that brought me to the top of a mountain in North Carolina on Christmas Eve to say "I do." I had never even dared to hope that a man like my husband even existed, but here I was, getting to marry him. I knew, with all my heart, that I was loved for who I was, not for what I could offer. And yet, I made a quiet, subconscious agreement in my spirit that I needed to offer perfection to be worthy of my husband's love and to find purpose as a wife and stepmother.

This tacit agreement came on the heels of my father suddenly passing away two months before our wedding. One of the most grievous events of my life coincided with the most joyous. The juxtaposition of the two was startling and overwhelming. But I took it all "like a champ." To top it all off, I moved to a new city, changed churches, sold two homes, and moved into a new home with my now-husband and his two children, leaving behind my community of friends and family. Grief in losing a parent is an unexpected journey in and of itself, but combine that with all of those changes in my life, and I was more thoroughly overwhelmed than I had ever been. But, per my "motus operandi," the more difficult life became, the harder I ran and the tighter I gripped onto trying to manufacture some sense of control and to find my purpose in perfection. Even in the face of so much upheaval, I was determined to be the consummate wife and stepmom.

And so, I returned to an idol who had long been my companion—self-reliance. Worshipping at the altar of autonomy felt good. It felt comfortable. I felt strong and in control of chaos, and as though I could outrun and outpace my fear of being a disappointment. I was stalwart in the face of the complexities that come with not only being a stepmom but also a wife to someone who had experienced betrayal. What is my role, exactly, with my husband's children? How do I interact with my step-children's mother and my husband's ex-wife? How can I be present for the kids without harming them in ways they have been hurt before? How do I avoid triggering old wounds in my husband's heart from his previous marriage? How do I manage my needs so I'm not too "demanding"? How do I reconcile feeling like too much and not enough? The questions seemed unanswerable and incessant, and the intricacies were staggering.

We live in a world where "strength is a virtue" and "what doesn't kill you makes you stronger." Cultural values would tell us that the goal is to be strong and self-sufficient—to have "nerves of steel" and an "unshakable spirit." What if we turn that upside down and embrace weakness in our story? What if we invite the paradox created in 2 Corinthians 12:9–10? Paul says, "And He said to me, 'My grace is sufficient for you, for My strength is made perfect in weakness.' Therefore, most gladly I will rather boast in my infirmities, that the power of Christ may rest upon me. Therefore, I take pleasure in infirmities, in reproaches, in needs, in persecutions, in distresses, for Christ's sake. For when I am weak, then I am strong" (NKJV). The kingdom of heaven is marked by these uncomfortable, upside-down tensions—to follow Christ is to live a paradox. We must live, while being called to die. In Christ's kingdom, the first are last. The least of these is greatest. We are children of the King of Kings and called to be servants of all. We are crucified with Christ, yet we live, or rather, He lives in us. So, can we welcome the tension created in Paul's invitation? Paul's proposition for us to embrace our weakness seems foreign. Even to our well-trained Christian hearts, the invitation to glory in our incompetency and heartache is wildly uncomfortable and feels foolish if lived out. But here we are, living in a burned-out society and sometimes in an even more pressure-ridden Church. We are entrenched in a culture of striving and appearing to have it all together. We want to feel as though we are in control. Suffering, pain, or even discomfort should be avoided. But when it inevitably comes, we press on with a plastered-on smile and a gut-wrenching determination to muster joy for Jesus. We live as though, "my strength is sufficient for me...my determination is enough to get me through anything, and I use pride and control to disguise my weaknesses."

Self-sufficiency is seductive, but it is a thief. Autonomy is an appealing but maladaptive way to self-soothe and attempt to feel in control, but it is a profound deception. It is intoxicating—laced with moments that create the illusion of control, but it blinds us to the reality that we are indeed weak, vulnerable, and insufficient. Whether it's a list of endless to-dos or a trial and hardship of immense magnitude, relying on ourselves corrodes our ability to trust God and creates a sense of urgency to simply rush through whatever we are facing. Autonomy is fertile soil for creating a sense of over-responsibility for people or circumstances over which we have no control. It can become insatiable when we believe that the success or failure of everything depends on our own strength and abilities. Self-sufficiency would also tell us that to need is to fail, or that experiencing "lack" is shameful. But, when we deny or even ignore our own needs, we further starve ourselves of experiencing one of the most beautiful facets of our Savior—His with-ness in our wants, and His capacity and desire to meet our needs. But that weakness and frailty that you try so hard to disguise, my dear friend, is a good thing—you were created for intimacy with God, and that intimacy is often cultivated through dependence. The deepest need in your soul is for God and for Him to provide Himself to you. Jesus says in John 15:5 (NIV), "I am the vine; you are the branches. If you remain in me and I in you, you will bear much fruit; apart from me, you can do nothing." Jesus holds all things together, and we are in desperate need of preaching that truth in our own hearts. One of my favorite ways to do this is through breath prayer—breathing in, I pray, "without You," breathing out, "I can do nothing." Can you speak kindly to yourself in this way? It is okay to be vulnerable and to need help. We are being formed and learning to rely on and abide in Jesus.

Perfection Is a Prison, Not a Purpose

I was 3 years into being a wife and stepmom, and I was wholly depleted. My chest was tight, and my breath was perpetually caught in my lungs, and my heart felt like a wasteland. Fear of failure and disappointing others ruminated in my heart. I wanted to prove to my husband that he had chosen well in a wife and a partner in raising his children. But no matter what I did or how well I did it, I felt constantly incompetent, anxious, depressed, and discouraged. Day by day and moment by moment, I chose to ignore the still small voice of God that offered me freedom, and the shackles of perfection wrapped themselves tighter around me as I turned inward for strength. I had been imprisoned by the perverted sense of purpose I sought by idolizing perfection. Every time I perceived that I came up short, I donned a mantle of shame that made my bones ache from the weight. I constantly felt like I was running up a mountain with a massive burden on my back, draped in a wet, weighted blanket while the trail behind me disappeared into a cavernous void. I was so weathered and so wounded by trying to fight the battle of perfection and shame that I collapsed to the ground in uncontrollable sobbing one evening while out on a walk with my husband. God had brought me to the end of myself, and there was no better place to be.

In my striving to offer perfection to my husband and to be the antithesis of the wicked stepmother, I actually ended up being the antithesis of what Jesus calls us to in Matthew 11:28–30 (NLT) when he says, "...Come to me, all of you who are weary and carry heavy burdens, and I will give you rest. Take my yoke upon you. Let me teach you, because I am humble and gentle at heart, and you will find rest for your souls. For my yoke is easy to bear, and the burden I give you is light." I had been so proficient at disguising self-reliance as strength and pride as resilience. But my needs, fragility, and my aching hunger for grace and rest gnawed at me. They were like echoes of a song that I had forgotten how to sing. But God was again meeting me in my barrenness of spirit—His love was an invitation to rest—to have the boundaries to say no when necessary and to express my needs, to not try and do and be all things for all people - to simply be me in all my very muchness and in all of my vulnerabilities.

I am wired to be long-suffering and proficient at enduring hardship. I am not often quick to recognize that

I am operating from a place of survival or trying to sustain myself with my own strength. Or, if I do recognize it, I am quick to dismiss it in favor of feeling as though I have some modicum of control in my life and to find my purpose in perfection. But, perfection, my dear friend, is not a purpose. It is a prison. You are not the answer to your own questions about your worth. Our worth, value, and purpose come from a far truer and deeper place than what we are able to do, produce, manufacture, or accomplish. So often, we either trust in our own sense of control, comfort, or identity, or we base our relationship with God on whether He gives us those things. But perfectionism will tear you asunder, leaving you heavy-laden and in profound need of the rest that Jesus offers. We need to trade the idea of "pressing on" for "pressing in"—pressing in closer to the heart of God who calls us to "Be still" and know him (Psalm 46:10, NIV). Pressing in towards God to lay down our strident pride so that we can know the truth of Exodus 14:14 (NIV), which says, "The Lord will fight for you, you need only to be still." Your purpose in life is not perfection—whether you feel like too much or not enough, your purpose is not bound to your feelings, nor is it contingent on your performance. We must preach this to ourselves daily and invite God into that searing wound so that He can meet our vulnerability with truth.

Making Space for Grace and Meeting God in the Middle

There is a price to idolizing self-sufficiency and perfectionism as reflections of our worth. The toll and stress that result from living out of our own strength are costly to all facets of our humanity—spirits, hearts, minds, and bodies. Disruptions or discomfort come, and we try desperately to minimize the damage. Suffering coils around us, and we frantically try to control anything and everything we can so as not to feel helpless or hopeless. But, my dear friend, disruptions, discomforts, and even suffering are inevitable. Our weaknesses and frailties are inescapable. But when we affix our worth or our well-being to how perfectly we navigate our lives, we allow ourselves to be robbed of an intimacy that God longs to have with us. When we grip control so tightly that we are unable to receive the fullness of life and joy that Jesus offers, we leave no room for grace, and we easily miss opportunities to cultivate a dependence on Him. Take a moment here and breathe—open your hands and release your striving so that you can receive grace-filled rest.

Every day, we are given the beautiful opportunity to turn towards hope and move towards the truth that God is not an absent bystander in our lives. Not to simply cross our fingers and hope it all works out, but to have a confident assuredness that God will redeem even the most grievous heartache for His glory and for our good. The hope in our struggle is not that we will have an easy life, but a life that is rich in experiencing the fullness and generosity of God's grace. Embracing our weaknesses as a vessel for God's strength takes the work of the Holy Spirit within us. Our sufferings, needs, and vulnerabilities are a severe mercy. They are a staunch but gentle teacher who, if we heed them, lead us closer to the heart of God. Jeremiah 17:7–8 (NKJV) gives us this gracious promise, "Blessed is the man who trusts in the Lord, and whose hope is the Lord. For he shall be like a tree planted by the waters, which spreads out its roots by the river, and will not fear when heat comes; But its leaf will be green, and will not be anxious in the year of drought, nor will it cease from yielding fruit." When we are rooted in Jesus, drawing nourishment from Him rather than trying to manufacture it ourselves, we can be strong and resilient, and He can live and love through us.

So, here I am, a stepmother and a wife in desperate need of the redemption of my strivings and a re-creation of my failings as avenues for grace. I am a stepmom and a wife who is frail and broken, whose wounds are deep and whose healing is ongoing. I am a stepmom and a wife choosing to look for threads of mercy and grace woven into my weakness as I lean into the strength of Jesus. I am a stepmom and a wife who is seeking to offer all the fractured and mangled pieces of my heart to a God who restores, renews, and redeems. I am a stepmom and a wife who still struggles with believing that I can and must be strong, self-reliant, and perfect. I am a stepmom and a wife, being mercifully untethered from my bondage to those things. To rely fully on God's strength in my weakness is not a one-and-done thing. It is a daily abandoning of my own pretense towards autonomy and a daily cultivation of reliance on Jesus. God calls my weakness good because it is in that beautifully dependent place that He is strong. I do not have to carry everything. I do not have to feel utterly shaken and ashamed when I fail. I do not have to fear the existence and expression of my needs. Instead, I rest in the arms of my Savior and am myself carried.

And so, my dear friend, we would do well to turn our attention to the circumstances that highlight our weakness and ask God to meet us there. To cultivate habits that allow our attention to be captive to our need for Him, and for His grace in us. Opportunities to be dependent on Jesus and to experience the richness of God's grace do not often occur in our gentle beginnings or in epic conclusions. God is most quietly and powerfully at work in the middle of our stories, and it is easy to miss Him if we do not intentionally seek Him out. We ask for His blessing at the start of things, and we often long for Him on the other side of difficulties, but we neglect to see Him in the middle or in the margins—in the disruption, the dailiness of living, the moment-by-moment situations that bid us turn to Him and to trust Him for grace and strength. We can live with the hopeful expectation that God is at work, like a potter, shaping and sanctifying you in ways that make you more like Jesus and equipping you to contribute to the kingdom of heaven. He is composing a masterpiece in and through you. May our imaginations be captivated by this beautiful realization—God is not finished with us. He wants to show Himself strong on our behalf, so that we can grow in knowing and loving Him more deeply and uniquely reflecting His glory to a broken world.

If your spirit feels any inkling towards perfection or striving in self-sufficiency, I invite you into awareness. I invite you to be a human being, not a human doing. Open your hands to receive His love and to lay down all of your aching and strivings to receive more of Him. Welcome to a space to have your heart poured into, with a blessing and a benediction. May you offer your needs, vulnerabilities, weaknesses, and hardships as spaces where grace and compassion flourish. May they be fruitful gardens where God's strength and lovingkindness nourish you. May you find yourself hidden and held in Jesus. May you honor your aching and tired heart, and may it be an indicator that you cannot do all things and be all things to all people. May any fears that have driven you to believe that there is no respite be obliterated by the truth that our Good Shepherd longs to lead us to green pastures and quiet waters. May the lies whispered to you by shame be shattered on the rock of truth. May the endless and unspeakably beautiful mercy of our Savior meet you in the darkest places of your heart. May your spirit reverberate with the freedom to be broken and imperfect because we have a healing Savior. May you bring your weariness as an offering and your emptiness as a vessel in which God can fill you with Himself. May your inadequacies be an invitation to spread your arms out in a welcome embrace of all that you are not so that all of who Jesus is can live, love, and flow through you. Amen.

Application and Next Steps

Here are a few things to help you as you begin to learn to surrender perfection and renew grace and dependency in your life.

1. Remember, God is in the middle of writing your story. You are unfinished. Look for what He is doing.

   - Begin your day with a prayer to have your eyes opened and heart softened to His work in and through you.

- Have a hope moment in the middle of your day—what, where, or with whom do you see Him working?

- Reflect on a moment of redemption from your day when you go to bed. Draw your attention to a moment where you saw God at work, where He revealed Himself to you.

- Trace His work and faithfulness back through the deserts and promised lands that He has already led you through.

2. Cultivate an awareness of God's desire to meet you in your weaknesses so that He can demonstrate His power and strength through you and so that you can cultivate dependency on Him.

   - Choose an area or situation in your life where you might be struggling and intentionally move towards God with open hands. Offer your entitlement for control and comfort to Him in this area, and let the posture of your heart be one of humility and hopeful expectation of what He will do when you give Him the pen in the story.

   - Set reminders for yourself to draw your attention to your need for God. Set God's truth before your eyes. For example, sticky notes on the mirror, using a cue like doing the dishes to be intentional in reminding yourself of your dependency on God, or practicing viewing moments of frustration or struggle as God's invitation to you to turn towards Him so He can be your sustainer.

3. Identify an area in your life where you feel like you have to be perfect, or like you have to control every facet of it.

   - Asking yourself some questions can be helpful here: Are there any areas that make you shudder or wince when you think about releasing control of them? Is there something in your life to which you are tying your worth and value? Whether chronic or short-term, are there any areas of your life that leave you feeling worthless if you do not meet your own expectations, or the expectations that you perceive others have of you?

   - Preach the gospel to yourself daily and have a clear understanding that you are not perfect—that God is masterfully piecing together all of your brokenness to gloriously reflect Him and draw you into deeper intimacy with Him.

   - Ask a spouse or trusted friend what areas they see in you that might be a blind spot with regard to perfectionism, or an area where you are trying to exert control and be self-sufficient. Ask them what their experience of you is when you are struggling. Ask them to help hold you accountable. With humility, ask them if they would point out any specific perfectionistic or controlling behaviors to you in the moment. Be willing to receive their feedback.

   - Once that area is identified, create a plan or system for how you will practice releasing control or surrendering your drive for perfection.

For example, when I feel that drive for autonomy in a certain area, often, my husband steps in and takes over whatever task I am doing, so I can step aside for a few minutes to take some deep breaths, pray, or move my body to release emotional energy.

- Choose an area of your life where that is particularly rife with the tendency to control and intentionally choose to release it to someone else, or to invite someone in to partner with you in it. Cultivate a daily rhythm of surrendering control or the drive to be perfect.

- Speak graciously to yourself as you would to your spouse, child, or dear friend. You would not expect perfection from them, so why be so harsh with yourself when you perceive you have failed? Speak the truth of your belovedness and worth in Jesus simply because you are a child of God.

4. Identify an area or situation in your life where you are having difficulty expressing your needs.

   - Remind yourself throughout the day that to need is to grow. And that Jesus longs to meet your needs with Himself or through something or someone else as a provision for you in your walk with Him.

   - Remember that not all needs are readily apparent or surface-level. For example, you might need help with folding laundry. Maybe you are overwhelmed by the task, or maybe your deeper need is support and/or a comforting connection with your spouse in a tedious chore.

- Practice asking for what you need. What is an area where you feel like you have to be self-sufficient and not ask for what you need? A helpful way to do this is to choose an area of your life where the stakes are low, or where you could easily accomplish the task yourself. Instead, choose to ask for help. For example, delegate a task to your spouse or to a colleague at work that you might have otherwise taken on yourself.

- Be generous with giving yourself grace and allowing yourself to receive it from others. Do not let your pride rob someone else of the opportunity to love you and bless you.

Chapter 8

Carried When I Could Not Stand: A Widow's Journey Through Betrayal, Mercy, and Divine Restoration

by Rita Dunham

He was gone, and there was absolutely nothing I could do that would ever bring him back. That's just not how it works. We are put here on this earth for a particular time, reason, and season...until God calls us home. My husband had transitioned, and I was thrust into a world that I never imagined could be so cold. Walking the path of a widow—an unbelievably difficult voyage riddled with struggle, and a deep sacrifice dedicated to trying to care for our children all on my own. All the time drawing from a tank that had been emptied long ago—when he told me he loved me for the final time, then glanced up at the ceiling and back at me as he mouthed the last precious words I would ever read from his lips. Words I will never forget as I looked into his eyes, as his voice slowly dwindled away, and I heard him say, "God is good." He looked at me in sorrow with tears in his eyes, then whispered, "I'm sorry."

At that point, the pain in my heart was so heavy I felt my entire body go numb from shock. It was at that very moment that my life changed in an instant. The unbelievable toll and weight it would take to care for our children, and one with a medical condition, took me to a place I never thought I would ever come back from.

The weight of having to process that in and of itself, not to mention having to bear it all on my own, left an indelible scar that will never fully heal. An extra layer of grief to an already gaping wound. But by the grace of God, He carried us even when we didn't have the strength to carry ourselves, and I am forever grateful. From the outpouring of compassion from several people who witnessed our struggle in an unfamiliar territory, without any immediate family, to those who were there during the dark days and endless nights.

I was grateful for what little we did have, and I had to take the broken pieces of yesterday and build back what was left of our lives, all while limping through the entire process, drawing from an empty tank. Finding the strength to comfort my children through this unspeakable disaster felt like carrying the weight of the world on my shoulders in addition to the unsympathetic who often viewed our situation as an opportunity to exploit our struggle in hopes of gaining whatever they could. And although I had to leave my job in order to focus on the needs of my family and juggle all of the demands of a widowed single mother, I held on to my side hustle as a business entrepreneur that allowed me to take a break from my regular nine-to-five during this gigantic storm in my life.

This was indeed a blessing that, unfortunately, many viewed as just another opportunity to exploit the situation and collect as much currency as they could through a multitude of schemes. There is no possible way on earth that I could have ever maintained my sanity and held it together had it not been for God Almighty carrying me at a time when I was already broken and carrying others just as fragmented from this massive upheaval. I will never forget the day my business partner called to inform me that a client had swindled me out of everything and bankrupted my entire enterprise, and the little I had left.

I had so many legal experts advising me to take litigation for recompensation to make up for the loss and hold on to my financial investment. However, this was not an easy decision to make because although I was in a financial strain, the steps I would have had to take would have put the client who also had a complicated family situation and more than likely would not have been able to withstand under the struggle that I had withstood, which would have also put them in a financial situation that they probably could not have even survived it like I had. God had given me the strength, protection, and wherewithal to get back up—even though my situation was rough. Which caused me to think and pray. Then something touched my heart and spirit with a powerful, thought-provoking revelation. It was as if I could suddenly start envisioning the possible detriment that would come their way had I moved forward to compensate all that was taken from my family and me— had I rightfully stood up on my own behalf to get back all that had been taken from me, even if it did, in turn, drain their resources like they had drained mine.

However, a heaviness and urgent sense of discernment came over me, and, in my conscience, it was almost as though I could see their possible destruction, and, in my heart, I knew I could not go through with taking legal action—even though I had every right to. Nevertheless, it would be revealed to me two years later and manifest in a much-needed rescuing situation that was worth a thousand times more than what I had sacrificed, as it came back to me for my own family in a way that I could never even capture or explain in a thousand words, even if I had tried. What we had experienced was nothing short of a true miracle. My only possible explanation is that God had opened up a window of a blessing that my mind could not explain nor conceive.

Even though I had witnessed so many blessings, setbacks, and struggles, I was still feeling a little down and out, and I needed a true friend, but who could I trust? I must admit it was one of the most difficult times of my life. I even found myself asking God, "Why me?" over and over again. Hadn't I always tried to be a good person and help others whenever I could? So why was this happening to me? What did I do to ever deserve this? Then one day, an old friend called, someone I hadn't heard from in years.

"How's it going?" My heart skipped a beat when I heard the sound of her voice on the other end.

"Wow, it's been such a long time, Cassandra. Is that you? What's up?" I couldn't believe my ears as a wave of relief washed over me, rejoicing in the fact that someone had cared enough to reach out in my time of need and that I finally had an acquaintance to face the tremendous struggle of what had become my life.

"Let's just say if I told you all that hadn't gone wrong, it'd be a much shorter story."

"Trust me, I definitely get it. This life can be so unpredictable, to say the least... I tried calling several times, but I kept getting the same message that the number was no longer in service."

"Oh no, sorry about that, but unfortunately, I had to change my phone number. The old one is no longer in service because I lost my device during all of the moving around, which contained all my stored contacts. You know I'm out here on my own, away from everyone... no family or friends."

"Oh my goodness, you must have really been having a hard time. I just wish you had reached out to me sooner... you know I would have had your back."

"I know you would have, but it's like my mind just went completely blank from all of the stress, and I couldn't remember anything."

"So where are you now?"

"I'm in a one-room rental unit for now until I can get back on my feet."

"Tell me where you are, I wanna come see you."

"Oh, please do, that would be so nice...I really do need a friend right now, and I really feel like just completely giving up."

"No-no-no, please don't talk like that, you know I got you and always have."

"Bless you." I rambled off the address as fast as I could as a wave of relief washed over me at the idea that someone was finally coming to help...that someone actually cared, and I wasn't alone anymore.

It was a beautiful sunny day as I waited outside on the front stoop for my bestie to arrive. The world looked so much brighter with someone in my corner, and I hadn't been totally forsaken. I basked in the tranquility and calm of nature as I watched the beautiful birds flutter among the lush landscape, trees, in joyous anticipation as Cassandra peddled toward me on a vintage 10-speed in vibrant colors.

"Finally!" I hopped off the bench and ran toward her as she anchored the kickstand on the bicycle, and we embraced in celebration.

"Wow, how you've changed..." She took a few steps back, staring in dismay as she took in my baggy jeans and oversized tee-shirt, taken aback by my disheveled appearance.

"Life..." I glanced hopelessly at her lean physique and sparkly workout apparel. I can see that life has certainly been good to you, though." I smiled despite the horror in her eyes.

"You just look..." She struggled to find the right words.

"Drained?" I quickly filled in the blank.

"I just wasn't expecting you to be…"

"This worn out, I guess." I could barely hold back the tears.

"Oh, I wouldn't say that." She placed her hand on my shoulder.

"Well, it's true… between trying to process becoming a widow and managing all of the pressure that fell on me caring for my children all alone in an unfamiliar place, with no immediate family, it finally all came crashing down at once."

"It's okay." She reached for my hand as we walked back toward the park bench.

"We're all doing fine now, I have a really good support system from the local church, and we're just trying to get back to as close to normal as we possibly can, although things will never again be the same."

"Just know that I'm here if you ever need a friend." She pulled out a slip of paper and tore it in half as we exchanged phone numbers and then parted ways.

It was six months later when I finally received the glorious call that the funding had come through to revamp my start-up business. I could barely contain the excitement as I signed the contract and relaxed in my beautiful new home, then quickly reached for my cell phone and pulled out the crumpled-up paper with Cassandra's phone number to share the good news.

"I'm sorry, ma'am, but I think you have the wrong number." I listened in devastation to the unfamiliar voice on the other side as the line disconnected. It was at that very moment that I realized that she had obviously regarded herself as superior to me because of my struggle. It seemed disheartening at first until I looked around at my beautiful surroundings. God had restored everything that had been lost and doubled what had been. My heart skipped a beat when I looked back at where He brought me from, as a broken spirit to the CEO of a major enterprise that was worth twice the investment I had lost.

Then it dawned on me that God, in His infinite wisdom, knew this was never a true friendship and not only did He reveal it, but He protected me from holding on to a relationship I once deemed trustworthy—when it was never to be trusted. As I looked back in deep reflection, I suddenly realized that if things had not worked out the way that they did, I may have taken an unreliable component on my journey who did not have good intentions. I may have unknowingly let my guard down to an extent that could have caused far more damage in the long run than the initial betrayal itself.

God had worked it out for the greater good. I smiled to myself as I sat back on my beautiful deck in the glistening sun, reveling in His magnificent glory, watching the children play in the luxurious backyard. It was truly a beauty out of darkness.

For years, I struggled endlessly, trying to find closure and comprehend how and why God, in all His holiness, would allow so much suffering and pain. Then, over time and through a lot of studying the Word, the answer suddenly came to me that no human being on earth would ever fully understand God. He is above and beyond our full comprehension and understanding, which finally made total sense to me because when I looked at it from the standpoint and fact that we serve an almighty God who gave His life and allowed Jesus, who was Himself in the flesh, to suffer for mankind...a world that He knew would ultimately betray Him. This is clear evidence that His ways are not our ways, and mankind will never be able to ever fully figure him out.

Even though it still baffles me to this very day, it leads me to an understanding that because of man's free will, there will always be suffering in this world and in this life. This knowledge has helped me to process things beyond my understanding and not take it personally when things go wrong or when I am mistreated, because God understands our suffering and hardships. We serve a God that understands what it feels like to be taken advantage of, betrayed, and ostracized. The brutal sacrifice that He made for this world brings a certain peace and understanding on even some of the toughest of days. And the more I prayed when things went wrong, the closer He drew me when I began to see things from an entirely different perspective. Even when I encountered unfairness and things that caused me to suffer that I didn't deserve, I didn't take it to heart like I used to.

It didn't affect me the same because I understood that everyone is on a different frequency and level of faith. Some are on a deeper level than others, and some are just beginning. Nevertheless, we are all still learning and growing. This concept not only strengthened my faith but also lessened the sting of betrayal, even though not always easy to accept. Then I looked up one day and realized that my whole world had changed...I could breathe easier, trusting in His timing and His will. Although when my husband transitioned, it felt like I had lost my identity.

It was like I kept asking myself, "Who am I?" After years of being married, connected to my soulmate and the beautiful moments we made together, which I will never forget as they continue to play over and over in my mind, even now, years later. Irreplaceable, precious moments from the unforgettable joy when we first learned that we had conceived, to the unparalleled delight when we welcomed each of our beautiful children into the world... a beautiful girl and a handsome boy.

The glorious adventure from the early days of changing diapers, baby baths, and snuggling and loving and caring for my family as a devoted mother and wife, all came crashing down into an entirely different world when I became a widow. A world filled with unspeakable heartache and grief. It was such a drastically different way of life that I almost didn't know who I was anymore. It was as though I had lost my place and identity in life...and there was no way back. Giving up was not an option, although I definitely felt like it. But I had to be strong for my children because I was all they had left...next to God.

The sadness in their eyes as they often looked around, longing for their father's return...wondering where he was and when he was coming back home was impossible to bear— especially since the only answer was "never." They didn't deserve it. We didn't deserve it—but deep inside, they knew.

*

About the
Authors

Robin Keahn Heim

obin Keahn Heim holds a Master of Arts in English and a Bachelor of Arts in Creative Writing. Now retired, she is fulfilling her lifelong goal of being a writer. Raised in Detroit, Michigan, she now lives in Southern California with her husband, Ernie, close to their family. She is slowly learning how to love the desert through the art of Georgia O'Keeffe. Her writing draws on her own experience of non-traditional families, ancestry research, and how language uncovers and decodes the presence of Post Traumatic Stress Disorder (PTSD), not often associated with women facing downward mobility.

Connect with Robin:

Email: keahn@hotmail.com

Substack: https://substack.com/@keahn

Laurie Knudsen

Laurie Knudsen shares her story of being sexually abused by her father as a young girl, coming to a head at the age of sixteen. She shares how she went from thinking God didn't care about her to being able to forgive her father. This allowed her to truly heal and move on with her life. She now lives in Omaha, Nebraska, where she is involved in her church and shares her story of hope and healing, as she is led. She enjoys time with her family, especially her five grandchildren.

Connect with Laurie:

Website: https://gatherinthesilence.com/

Laura Lee Pettit

aura Lee Pettit was born and raised in the Chicago area, met her husband in childhood, and they've been together 40+ years. They followed God's leading to Colorado, living within walking distance of their daughter, son-in-law (truly a son), and step-grandson. Laura has long written quietly for herself. She's a reader, a journal writer, a lifelong learner, a deep listener, enjoys laughing, encouraging others, and sharing life. She believes in the power of prayer, healing, wholeness, and walking in victory with Jesus. Through her words, she hopes to remind others they are not alone.

Connect with Laura:

Website: https://lauraslines.home.blog/

Kristi May

Kristi May resides in Lancaster County, Pennsylvania, with her husband, Ben, and their dog, Oreo. She is an entrepreneur, writer, and consultant who finds joy in encouraging others toward growth and hope. Kristi loves exploring how God speaks through everyday stories and believes that even small steps of faith can reshape a life. When she's not working with clients or writing, you'll find her enjoying good conversations or time with her family and friends.

Connect with Kristi:

Instagram: https://www.instagram.com/kristi_cherie/

LinkedIn: https://www.linkedin.com/in/kristin-may/

Elizabeth Bass

Elizabeth Bass is a 67-year-old mother of five adult children, and "Memae" to eleven energetic and precious grandchildren. She resides in Madison, WI, with her very best friend and husband, Clifford, and her service dog, Tobi. She enjoys many forms of crafting: sewing, painting, mosaics, pottery, glass fusing, and especially knitting. Her passion is to make things to give away. If she blesses the heart of a person with a special gift made specifically for them, she is overjoyed! Although she is on the razor's edge of learning to use technology, she is very gradually acclimating to it.

Connect with Elizabeth:

Website: https://www.themanyofme.com/

Website: https://manyofme-rebirthed.site/

Elaine Lopez

Elaine Lopez is a new writer and poet passionate about helping women navigate the intersection of faith and domestic abuse. After surviving a toxic, abusive relationship, she spent years finding healing through scripture and a profoundly life-altering encounter and understanding of God's love. She is a co-collaborator in the My Hope Story Volume 2, a memoir that encourages readers to stop hiding from their darkest pain and start facing it with hope in Jesus Christ. Elaine Lopez lives in Cherry Hill, New Jersey, with her family.

Connect with Elaine:

Facebook: https://www.facebook.com/lainey.lane.5

AnnaGrace Head

AnnaGrace Head is a paralegal and classically trained violinist whose life is a compendium of reason and creativity. A wife and stepmother, she writes from within the complexities of blended family life, attending to its fractures, nuances, and its beauty. Her love of writing began in college through journaling, where words became a means of prayer and an outlet for processing. Rooted in the belief that in Jesus there is grace upon grace, her work seeks to breathe life into its readers, offering the quiet assurance of being seen, known, and held in a shared sense of with-ness.

Connect with AnnaGrace:

Instagram: https://www.instagram.com/agstrange/

Rita Dunham

Rita Dunham is a strong-willed overcomer who has withstood a multitude of life challenges, strengthening her faith and determination. Growing up under the guidance of a strong Christian matriarch, she learned early on in life the power that came with leaning on God and was encouraged to follow her creative passion for writing from early childhood. A career she pursued that led her on the path of a feature columnist and a multitude of writing projects.

After experiencing several loved ones' transitions, including her spouse, she found herself hurled into a world often filled with trials and hardship that left her no other choice but to lean on the faith that had been instilled in her from youth, which produced a strong resilience in the face of a multitude of setbacks. She truly enjoys encouraging others.

Connect with Rita:

Facebook: https://www.facebook.com/rita.dunham.549

Closing

Dear Reader,

Thank you for reading *My Hope Story Vol. 2*!

I want to take a moment to celebrate the incredible authors who contributed to this meaningful book. They have poured their hearts into discovering, clarifying, and sharing their unique messages—and now, you get to benefit from their hard work and dedication.

At hope*books, we are deeply proud of our authors and are honored to partner with them on this journey. If you've ever considered writing and publishing your book, we invite you to visit hopebooks.com to learn more about our coaching and publishing services. We believe that everyone has a message to share and an audience to serve, and the world needs your hopeful words now more than ever.

Once again, let's take a moment to celebrate the hard work of these authors in bringing *My Hope Story Vol. 2* to life.

Sincerely,

Brian Dixon
Publisher, hope*books

Endnotes

Chapter 1

1. van der Kolk, Bessel. *The Body Keeps the Score: Brain, Mind, and Body in the Healing of Trauma.* Penguin, 2015.

2. TerKeurst, Lysa. *Forgiving What You Can't Forgive.* Nelson, 2020.

3. Heim, Robin. "Autobiography as Self-Defense in the Works of Agnes Newton-Keith and Michelle Kennedy." *Master's thesis*, California State University, San Bernardino, 2010, pp. 5–6, 23–26, 63–68, 94.

4. Warren, Elizabeth, and Amelia Warren Tyagi. *The Two-Income Trap: Why Middle-Class Mothers and Fathers Are Going Broke.* Bask Books, 2003.

Chapter 2

1. "Hope." *Dictionary.net*, Dictionary.net LLC, 2026, https://www.dictionary.net/dictionary/hope. Accessed 17 Feb. 2026.

2. Stevenson, Mary. *"Footprints in the Sand." Poetseers. org*,https://www.poetseers.org/the-great-poets/ misc-2/footprints-in-the-sand/. Accessed 17 Feb. 2026.

3. *Something About Amelia.* Directed by Randa Haines, performances by Ted Danson and Roxanne Zal, ABC, 1984.

Chapter 7

1. Communion, C. (2023) *Commoners_Communion.* Available at: https://www.instagram.com/p/CnFe9 qny0Rh/?img_index=2 (Accessed: 2025).

2. *Snow White and the Seven Dwarfs.* Directed by David Hand, Walt Disney Productions, 1937.

Looking to *connect* with a
community of writers?

> The world needs your
> *hope-filled* words
> more now than ever before.

Thinking about *writing*
your own book?